Writing and Presenting a Business Plan

Managerial Communication Series

By **Carolyn A. Boulger**
University of Notre Dame

Series Editor: **James S. O'Rourke, IV**
University of Notre Dame

THOMSON
™
SOUTH-WESTERN

Australia · Brazil · Canada · Mexico · Singapore · Spain · United Kingdom · United States

THOMSON
™
SOUTH-WESTERN

Writing and Presenting a Business Plan, Managerial Communication Series
James S. O'Rourke, IV, series editor; Carolyn A. Boulger, author

VP/Editorial Director:
Jack W. Calhoun

VP/Editor-in-Chief:
Dave Shaut

Sr. Publisher:
Melissa Acuna

Acquisitions Editor:
Neil Marquardt

Developmental Editor:
Taney Wilkins

Sr. Marketing Manager:
Larry Qualls

Production Editor:
Robert Dreas

Manager of Technology, Editorial:
Vicky True

Web Coordinator:
Karen Schaffer

Manufacturing Coordinator:
Diane Lohman

Production House:
Lachina Publishing Services

Printer:
Transcontinental
Louiseville, Quebec

Art Director:
Stacy Shirley

Cover and Internal Designer:
Robb and Associates

Cover Images:
© Artville/Richard Cook

Library of Congress Control Number:
2005926063

For more information about our
products, contact us at:
Thomson Learning
Academic Resource Center
1-800-423-0563

Thomson Higher Education
5191 Natorp Boulevard
Mason, OH 45040
USA

This is for my family:
Pam, Colleen, and Jay, Molly, and Kathleen.
And, of course, our latest addition, Cianan.
It's for my colleages, as well:
Carolyn, Sandra, Cynthia, and Sondra.
Thanks for all you've done to make my life
meaningful, rich, and . . . busy.
JSO'R, IV

For my husband, Bill,
and my son, Adam.
Thank you for your unconditional
love and support.
CAB

AUTHOR BIOGRAPHIES

From 1997 to 2005, Carolyn A. Boulger, Ph.D., served as a professor of management and taught business and management communication courses, as well as entrepreneurship electives, to undergraduates and M.B.A. candidates in the Mendoza College of Business at the University of Notre Dame in South Bend, Indiana. She also taught online courses in business and strategic communication for not-for-profit organizations. Additionally, Professor Boulger served as an advisor to the Gigot Center for Entrepreneurial Studies, where she coached finalist teams of undergraduates, graduate students, and Notre Dame alumni in annual business plan competition events.

In June 2005, Professor Boulger was appointed Dean of Graduate Studies at the College of Notre Dame in Baltimore, Maryland. She now oversees eight graduate degree programs in business, liberal studies, and education. She is also the author of *e-Technology and the Fourth Economy* (South-Western College Publishing, 2003). Professor Boulger earned her Ph.D. in Mass Media from Michigan State University, her M.S. in Journalism from Columbia University, and her B.A. in Communications from Simmons College.

James S. O'Rourke teaches management and corporate communication at the University of Notre Dame, where he is Founding Director of the Eugene D. Fanning Center for Business Communication and Concurrent Professor of Management. In a career spanning four decades, he has earned an international reputation in business and corporate communication. *Business Week* magazine has twice named him one of the "outstanding faculty" in Notre Dame's Mendoza College of business.

His publications include *Management Communication: A Case-Analysis Approach* from Prentice-Hall, now in second edition, and *Business Communication: A Framework for Success* from Thomson Learning. Professor O'Rourke is also senior editor of an eight-book series on Managerial Communication and is principal author or directing editor of more than 100 management and corporate communication case studies.

Professor O'Rourke is a graduate of Notre Dame with advanced degrees from Temple University, the University of New Mexico, and a Ph.D. in Communication from the S. I. Newhouse School of Syracuse University. He has held faculty appointments at the United States Air Force Academy, the Defense Information School, the United States Air War College, and the Communications Institute of Ireland. He was a Gannett Foundation Teaching Fellow at Indiana University in the 1980s, and a graduate student in language and history at Christ's College, Cambridge University in England during the 1970s.

Professor O'Rourke is a member and trustee of The Arthur W. Page Society, and a member of the Reputation Institute and the Management Communication Association. He is also a regular consultant to *Fortune 500* and mid-size businesses throughout North America.

TABLE OF CONTENTS

FOREWORD

In recent years, for a variety of reasons, communication has grown increasingly complex. The issues that seemed so straightforward, so simple not long ago are now somehow different, more complicated. Has the process changed? Have the elements of communication, or the barriers to success been altered? What's different now? Why has this all gotten more difficult?

Several issues are at work here, not the least of which is pacing. Information, images, events, and human activity all move at a much faster pace than they did just a decade ago. Among the more popular, hip new business magazines is a publication named *Fast Company*. Readers are reminded that it's not just a matter of tempo, but a new way of living we're experiencing.

Technology has changed things as well. We're now able to communicate with almost anyone, almost anywhere, 24/7, with very little effort and very little professional assistance. It's all possible because of cellular telephone technology, VOIP, digital imaging, the Internet, fiber optics, global positioning satellites, teleconferencing codecs, high-speed data processing, online data storage, and . . . well, the list goes on and on. What's new this morning will be old hat by lunch.

Culture has intervened in our lives in some important ways. Very few parts of the world are inaccessible any more. Other people's beliefs, practices, perspectives, and possessions are as familiar to us as our own. And, for many of us, we're only now coming to grips with the ideas that our own beliefs aren't shared by everyone and that culture is hardly value-neutral.

For a thousand reasons, we've become more emotionally accessible and vulnerable than ever before. You may blame Oprah or Jerry Springer for public outpouring of emotions, but they're not really the cause—they're simply another venue for joy, rage, or grief. The spectacle of thousands of people in London mourning at the death of Diana, Princess of Wales, took many of us in the United States by surprise. By the time the World Trade Center towers came down in a terrorist attack, few of us had tears left to give.

The nature of the world in which we live—one that's wired, connected, mobile, fast-paced, iconically visual, and far less driven by logic—has changed in some not-so-subtle ways in recent days. The organizations that employ us and the businesses that depend on our skills now recognize that communication is at the center of what it means to be successful—and at the heart of what it means to be human.

To operate profitably means that businesses must now conduct themselves in responsible ways, keenly attuned to the needs and interests of their stakeholders. And, more than ever, the communication skills and capabilities we bring to the workplace are essential to our success, both at the individual and at the societal level.

So, what does that mean to you as a prospective manager or executive in training? For one thing, it means that communication will involve more than simple writing, speaking, and listening skills. It will involve new contexts, new applications, and new technologies. Much of what will affect the balance of your lives has yet to be invented. But when it is, you'll have to learn to live with it and make it work on your behalf.

The book you've just opened is the eighth and final volume in a series that will help you to do all of those things and more. It's direct, simple, and very compact. The aim of my colleague and friend, Professor Carolyn Ann Boulger, is to pinpoint the issues and ideas most closely associated with successful new business ventures. "Remember," she told me, "that an idea is *not* a business, no matter how good it may be." In this volume, Professor Boulger shows us how to conduct a feasibility analysis, how to transform the results into a workable plan of action, how to seek funding for new ventures, and how to pitch your ideas successfully to angels, venture capitalists, and financial backers. She also asks the reader to examine the business idea from a stakeholder's perspective: What sustainable advantage does your plan bring to the marketplace, and how do you propose to turn that advantage into a profit-making business?

In the first volume in this series, Professor Bonnie Yarbrough of the University of North Carolina Greensboro examines issues related to *Leading Groups and Teams*. She reviews the latest research on small group and team interaction and offers practical advice on project management, intra-team conflict, and improving results.

In the series' second volume, the author of the book now in your hands, Professor Carolyn Boulger of Notre Dame, explores *e-Technology and the Fourth Economy*. With the help of renowned Swedish communication consultant Hans V. A. Johnsson, she looks at the emergence of a fundamental revolution in how people work, live, and earn a living. And she examines how the new technologies have influenced and transformed everything from commercial relationships to distance learning and more.

Professor Sandra Collins, who is the author of several books in this series, is a social psychologist by training. She has written *Communication in a Virtual Organization,* offering a conceptual framework to help you to understand how time and distance compression have altered work habits and collaboration. With the help of corporate communication executives and consultants, she documents exciting, current examples of global companies and local groups that illustrate the ways in which our work and lives have permanently changed.

She is also the author of *Managing Conflict and Workplace Relationships*. Her aim in that book is to pinpoint the issues and ideas most closely associated with managing both conflict and our day-to-day business relationships. Her approach involves far more than dispute resolution or determining how limited resources can be allocated equitably among people who all think they deserve more. She shows us how to manage our own emotions, as well as those of others. Creative conflict, organizational harmony, and synchronicity in the workplace are issues that too many of us have avoided simply because we didn't understand them or didn't know what to say.

For the iconically challenged (I am one who thinks in words and phrases, not pictures), Notre Dame professor Robert Sedlack and Northwestern University professor Barbara Shwom examine *Graphics and Visual Communication for Managers*. If you've ever wondered how to transform words and numbers into pictures, they can help. And for all of us who've ever tried to explain complex issues without success, either aloud or on paper, the message is simple: If you can't say it in a clear, compelling way, perhaps you can show them.

The penultimate volume in the series features Professor Sandra Collins exploring the psychological processes involved in *Listening and Responding*. There she helps us to understand why listening is more than an involuntary physical process, but a complex and difficult psychological process that requires commitment, energy, and understanding. Knowing when and how to seek and give feedback can make a relationship more productive and an organization more functional. Of all the communication skills we possess as humans, few can be more important than listening to and understanding what others are trying to say. With Professor Collins's help, you can become not only better at understanding others, but more adept at influencing their views and behaviors.

This is an interesting, exciting, and highly practical series of books. They're small, of course, intended not as comprehensive texts, but as supplemental readings or as stand-alone volumes for modular courses or seminars. They're engaging because they've been written by people who are smart, passionate about what they do, and more than happy to share what they know. And I've been happy to edit the series, first, because these authors are all friends and colleagues whom I know and have come to trust. Second, I've enjoyed the task because this is really interesting stuff. Read on. There is a lot to learn here, new horizons to explore, and new ways to think about human communication.

James S. O'Rourke, IV
The Eugene D. Fanning Center
Mendoza College of Business
University of Notre Dame, Notre Dame, Indiana

Managerial Communication Series
Editor: James S. O'Rourke, IV

The **Managerial Communication Series** is a series of modules designed to teach students how to communicate and manage in today's competitive environment. Purchase only this module as a supplemental product for your Business Communication, Management, or other Business course, or purchase all eight modules, packaged together at a discounted price for full coverage of Managerial Communication.

ISBN: **0-324-15254-X**

This text reviews the latest research on small group and team interaction, and offers practical advice on project management, intra-team conflict, and improving results. It contains group and team worksheets, progress reports, and sample reporting instruments, as well as classroom discussion questions and case studies.

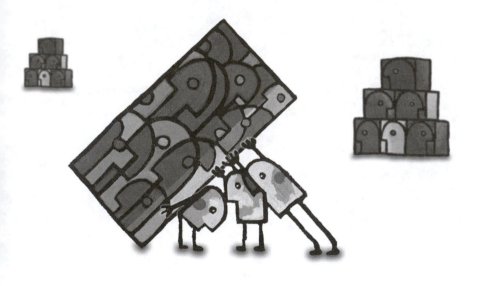

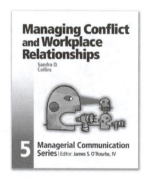

ISBN: **0-324-15257-4**

Learn what social scientists and business executives now know about conflict, personality style, organizational structure, and human interaction. Examine the most successful strategies for keeping your edge and keeping your friends. Practical forms, instruments, and applications are included.

Contact your local Thomson Representative at 800-423-0563. Or visit the series Web site at **http://orourke.swlearning.com** *for more product information and availability.*

ISBN: 0-324-15255-8

This text offers a radical new view of technology's impact on what the author calls "The Fourth Economy," an economic model based entirely on minds in interaction. Technology's role in helping participants in the radically transformed landscape of the twenty-first century is not limited to the transmission and storage of text and data, but extends to the very ways in which people think about and create value.

ISBN: 0-324-15256-6

This text explores the risks and opportunities open to those who work in new alliances, partnerships, and non-traditional business models. A look at both theory and practical application offers students and managers the chance to observe successful organizations in action. Foreword by Sixtus J. Oeschle of Shell Oil and Internet Pipeline.

ISBN: 0-324-16178-6

This text offers some practical and useful advice on how to work with graphics and visuals in reports, briefings, and proposals. It also offers direct instruction on how to integrate graphic aids into spoken presentations and public speeches. If you can't say it or write it clearly, you may be able to show it. Dozens of illustrations, drawings, and graphs are included.

ISBN: 0-324-15258-2

This text examines the basis for culture, reviewing the work of social scientists, cultural anthropologists, and global managers on this emerging topic. Definitions of culture, issues of cultural change and how cultures adapt are included, along with practical examples, case studies, and illustrations of how cultural issues are managed both domestically and internationally.

ISBN: 0-324-30167-7

This text explores how successful companies and effective managers use listening as a strategic communication tool at all levels of the organization. Examples of how organizations have used listening techniques to resolve conflicts, build relationships with clients and employees, and adapt to maintain a competitive edge are discussed.

ISBN: 0-324-30168-5

This text reviews the entire process of writing and presenting a business plan. From idea generation to feasibility analysis, and from writing the plan to presenting it to various audience groups, this text covers all steps necessary to develop and start a business. It also offers guidance on meeting with investors and getting funding for the new venture, and provides numerous samples of effective plans and presentations.

INTRODUCTION

Perhaps the most important lesson to emerge from the electronic business collapse of 2001 is that entrepreneurs need well-thought-out, sustainable business models. Groceries by e-mail or rain gear for pets via the Internet somehow never caught on. No matter how interesting the entrepreneurial concept, without a tight, well-designed business model, the venture is unlikely to gain interest from the investment community. Today, that community is much more cautious than it was five or ten years ago. They now know that a poorly designed model rarely yields the anticipated performance outcomes. The financial community simply will not consider a venture that does not have a strong business model reflected in a well-written business plan.

Cynics have said that an entrepreneurial vision that cannot be executed is a hallucination. They may be right. A thoughtful, well-crafted business plan certainly increases the likelihood that a venture *can* be launched successfully and the resulting business *can* be sustained. As Carolyn Boulger shows us, the process of writing a business plan forces the entrepreneur to systematically think about the critical elements of a robust business model in a logical, comprehensive manner. A good business plan communicates the elements of the business model so that the vision, strategy, and tactics of the entrepreneur become clear to the investor and business partner.

Simply put, a good business plan is a living document that evolves with a dynamically competitive business environment. Such plans are really a snapshot, a point in time in the life of a business. Rationally comprehensive, long-term planning is a thing of the past. Dynamism and change are today's business reality. Entrepreneurs are change agents in an economy because they find and exploit opportunities missed by others. And it is the well-crafted business plan that helps an entrepreneur manage the risks associated with launching a new venture in an environment hostile toward new ideas and change of any sort.

An entrepreneurial business plan is more than a road map. It is a sales document. Its purpose is to sell a vision. It supports a business concept with reliable data and estimations. It demonstrates how the market will accept the product or service, that the market is large enough to merit the business, and that the concept is scalable. It also describes the business's revenue model and explains just how its founders, employees, and investors can expect a fair return on their investment. Finally, it provides milestones and financial plans necessary for launching the business.

Professor Boulger's book *Writing and Presenting a Business Plan* masterfully describes how an entrepreneurial plan must be written and communicated for a successful venture. She has worked closely with entrepreneurs, investment angels, and venture capitalists for many years and has mentored a number of successful start-ups through the planning and investment process. She has a keen understanding of the elements of a business model the investment community requires and the concrete business plan they demand. She has eloquently captured both in this book. Entrepreneurs will appreciate the clear and practical way in which she describes the planning process.

Professor Boulger has taught management communication with distinction at the University of Notre Dame for many years. This book reflects her experience and skill in communicating business ideas to students, to academics, to investors, to entrepreneurs, and to venture capitalists. Entrepreneurs may have revolutionary ideas—ideas with the potential to transform economies—but if they are unable to communicate those ideas, they will never see the light of day. Carolyn Boulger shows readers how to compose, organize, and present those ideas. Her background in communication, journalism, and economics clearly helps her demonstrate the best practices in business plan communication and design.

A Google search on "business-plan guides" will yield more than 11,300,000 hits. While there is no shortage of business planning tools on the market today, this book is unquestionably among the very best. Read on. Let Carolyn Boulger show you how you can realize your entrepreneurial dreams.

James H. Davis
Associate Professor of Management and Director
Gigot Center for Entrepreneurial Studies
University of Notre Dame, Notre Dame, Indiana

1

WHAT TO DO WITH THAT GREAT IDEA

"You can't think outside the box if you haven't learned to think inside it first."

Donald Trump

You know you can't cook, but you'd like to open a restaurant chain. Or you can't sew, but your dream is to turn retail fashion on its Manolo-clad heels. What's the answer? All you need to do is write up a business plan, hand it over to one of the many venture capitalists who have been patiently waiting for you to finish with "preliminaries," and you're good to go. With certified check in hand, you're off and running, launching your own business with assured success and a market that can't remember how it managed to get by before you blew into town.

Sure, that could happen. But it begs the question: If starting a business is so very easy, why doesn't everyone become an entrepreneur? After all, what could possibly be better than working for oneself? You can be your own boss, set your own hours, shape your own destiny—or so goes the rhetoric of the would-be self-employed and very, very wealthy.

Sounds like a good deal, at least on the surface. But why, then, does one of every two businesses fail within its first three years?[1] Perhaps it's in part because entrepreneurial folklore weaves a fantasy of perfection in pursuit of success, name dropping Michael Dell's and Bill Gates's anecdotes in its path. The finished product rather than the gritty process becomes the assumption, the expectation, and the norm.

Unfortunately, for most people, it's not the reality. The good news is that there are ways to greatly increase the odds that for you, it just might be.

This book is aimed at would-be entrepreneurs and business owners who hope to proactively improve the odds for long-term success though intensive focus on the steps involved in (1) developing a business idea; (2) conducting a feasibility study; (3) writing a business plan; and (4) presenting that plan to multiple audience groups. Each of the five chapters in this book tackles one of these challenges, featuring interviews with successful entrepreneurs and numerous examples of what really works at each stage of this process. This first chapter is devoted to the most instrumental elements of your potential success—your attitudes, expectations, experiences, and assumptions.

An essential first step is to figure out whether you are an entrepreneur or sole proprietor at heart. Do you dream of changing the world? Or do you want to work for yourself and realize personal success, making contributions on local or regional levels? There's a big difference but no right answer here. Both require persistence, a ton of work, good timing, financial backing, and a touch of luck. Nor are the two always mutually exclusive, as big dreams get localized and sole proprietors obtain success through franchise arrangements.

To place yourself in either the "entrepreneur" or "sole proprietor" camp, it's helpful to consider the following five question sets. They're open ended but can offer a lot of insight as to where your heart lies on this matter.

1. How do you handle change and risk? Is it important for you to be able to plan and execute activities without incident? How spontaneous are you? Is it essential for you to set and meet the same goals, or do you adapt goals as situations change?

2. If money were no object, what activities and accomplishments would make you the happiest and most proud? If you were to write your own obituary, what would you want it to say?

3. What life experiences—personal, professional, educational, spiritual, and emotional— have provided the most satisfaction and "sense of peace" so far in your life? List five in each category, and then pick one from each category and rank their impact on your perspective of life.

4. How important are control and routine to you? How important is the end versus the means? How necessary is it for you to control the elements that affect your daily, weekly, and monthly schedules? Your income? Your time away from work?

5. How well do you handle criticism? How have you reacted to past perceived failures? How do you define success?

Entrepreneurship is by its nature risky and spontaneous. You'll need to adapt to situations for which you may not have fully planned, and you certainly will be asked to multitask. The hours are notoriously long, so you had better be filling them with something you really enjoy. Because there are no guarantees, be sure that you are prepared to handle the process of building your business, not just its success. Lastly, do not become paralyzed by the possibility of failure. To be successful, you'll be required to learn from your mistakes and move forward, putting that experience to good use.

In general, entrepreneurs see and think past themselves and the present, envisioning possibilities well into the future. Sole proprietors tend to think about the impact of a new business on themselves, their partners, and their family members, measuring impact on a local rather than global scale. Either way, both begin with a mission and vision for how the business will enter and grow in its designated marketplaces. There are many ways to develop mission and vision statements, but first you need to know what product or service you have to offer and whether the marketplace really wants that product or service at this time.

It may seem obvious, but you also need to have basic skills in the business areas you hope to enter. If you can't cook and don't sew, you may wish to avoid restaurants and retail fashion. It simply doesn't work to solve your lack of relative and crucial experience by hiring the skill sets of others; you must possess them yourself to be credible with both investors and customers. It's fine to outsource services such as legal guidance, tax assistance, and accounting requirements, but it's best to possess the core competencies for which you expect compensation from your customers. This also is invaluable in identifying business opportunities disguised as problems to the untrained eye.

Start-up Profile: License Monitor

It was by identifying a problem that entrepreneur Mike Garvey found the premise for his now successful start-up company. Over the span of a decade, the former New York police officer pulled over more than 1,000 drivers of corporate-owned automobiles and trucks, many of whom had invalid driver's licenses. When these drivers were found at fault in accidents, the liability fell to their employers, who often were unaware of their drivers' invalid, suspended, or nonexistent licenses. Mike wondered why. A little research showed that companies with corporate fleets were legally required to verify employee driving records on only an annual basis. He also was appalled at what else he learned:

- Statistics prove that drivers with suspended licenses are *three times* more likely to kill or seriously injure others in collisions.
- One of five traffic fatalities involves a driver without a proper license.
- Lawsuits are piling up against companies whose employees—often unbeknownst to their employer—had a track record of reckless, dangerous driving.
- Seventy-five percent of drivers whose licenses have been suspended or revoked continue to drive.

After witnessing and researching these problems firsthand, Garvey decided to launch a business to help rectify the situation. His business proposition: that checking employees' motor vehicle department records at time of hire and once or twice a year is not adequate as a protection against corporate liability. Thanks to License Monitor, customers now know the status of their drivers at all times and are automatically updated when or if that status changes. The three-year-old company delivers twenty-four/seven protection through its Web portal, its interface with the Department of Motor Vehicles, and its ability to translate and then transfer complicated records concerning court convictions, accidents, alcohol- and drug-related driving incidents, expirations, restrictions, suspensions, revocations, and other activity related to employee driving records.

By all means, this is the time to think big. Begin with a magnificent end in mind. Sure, you'll likely need to downsize while you build back up to your goal, but do so with the understanding that the path to success is often neither direct nor without failure. As the founder and CEO of Pace Global Energy Services, LLC, Tim Sutherland spent twenty-five years building his international energy consulting, procurement, and risk management business to where it now has clients in more than forty countries on six continents. But he started small, with only $3,000, one U.S. government contract, and four partners in Fairfax, Virginia. Tim has watched his company grow to include regional offices in Houston, Columbia (South Carolina), Montreal, London, Mexico City, and Moscow, and his client list expand to energy developers, financial institutions, public utilities, and industrials. The company now manages more than $2 billion in energy contracts and $5 billion in financial portfolios on behalf of its clients, and it employs more than 200 energy professionals.

By his own admission, much of Tim's success came the hard way, by learning from his mistakes. "All of us make so many mistakes in the process of our lives, and many people are uncomfortable in saying that they made a mistake," says Sutherland. "Instead they try to rationalize it, to justify or lessen its impact. But I've learned that acknowledging a mistake is a good thing, not a recognition of an inherent flaw. I don't stand up and announce to the world, 'Hey folks, I made another one.' But it is very liberating to say you made a mistake and satisfying to figure out what you have learned from it."[2]

One of his earliest lessons: All ideas are not created equal. It is important to keep sight of your core competencies and realize that some "good ideas" for rapid growth opportunities may not be in the company's long-term best interest. "Access the expected value of the growth opportunity on its individual merits and how it relates to core competencies," cautions Sutherland. "The lack of alignment that fragmentation causes is very costly in so many ways."[3]

Not all good ideas make for good businesses, and not all good businesses are good choices for you, given your areas of expertise and experience. Understanding the mechanics of writing and presenting a business plan is not enough to succeed as an entrepreneur—success largely begins with the quality of the idea and the availability of market(s) to support it.

WHERE TO BEGIN: IDEA GENERATION

Good ideas are everywhere—you only need the appropriate lens to recognize them when you see them. Through the eyes of an entrepreneur, problems indeed present opportunities for new businesses. Presented next are eight options for generating vibrant ideas for new ventures. Combining these options also presents unique potential for generating numerous ideas for new businesses.

OPTION 1: USE THE PROBLEM/SOLUTION MODEL

Successful start-ups aren't accidental, but certainly, accidents can lead to successful start-ups. Many businesses begin out of frustration as the entrepreneur struggles to solve a problem or fulfill a need. Consider the story of 3M™. Founded in 1902 as a mining company, 3M has spent more than 100 years building successes out of short-term failures. The company was conceived to mine mineral deposits to create grinding-wheel abrasives. Lack of success in this venture prompted the five founders to refocus on a related product, sandpaper. Even then, it took years for the company to determine the appropriate balance between production and supply. Eventually, 3M evolved to become the creator of adhesives such as Scotch® tape, Scotchlite™ Reflective Sheeting for highway markings, magnetic sound recording tape, and Scotchgard™ Fabric Protector, to name only a few products of this now highly diverse and multibillion-dollar company. One of its more notable accidents occurred during the 1980s, when a 3M scientist used an adhesive that didn't stick to create "temporarily permanent" book markers—and a whole new product category—Post-it® Notes.[4]

Other problems that present options out of which entrepreneurial solutions may grow include a need for organizations to comply with government or industry regulations. That was the case for CN Resources, a national child nutrition consulting start-up firm based in Arizona. In developing his business, company president Rich Crandall recognized two unmet needs of organizations vying for dollars in the $50 billion child nutrition industry. Crandall knew that as a condition of accepting federal financial support, states would be required to complete mandatory paperwork and operational reviews, yet have limited human and financial resources to allocate to such tasks. Second, he recognized that the school districts and day-care centers ultimately receiving federal funds for children's meal programs would likely need help as well.

CN Resource was designed to meet those challenges by offering outsourced service alternatives for state agencies, school districts, and adult/child day-care centers. By specializing in two groups of narrow but essential services—compliance audits of federal government programs such as NSLP (National School Lunch Program) and CACFP (Child and Adult Care Food Program) and technical assistance to customers of these programs, such as school districts and day care centers—the company has been able to grow by at least 550 percent since its formation in 2002.

OPTION 2: APPLY TIME/MONEY FILTERS TO THE PROBLEM/SOLUTION MODEL

Time and money are two of our scarcest resources, with trade-offs between the two a common justification for many business models. How often do you purchase fast food at a drive-through window rather than cook at home or send clothes to the dry cleaners that could have been safely laundered? In examining your daily habits, which tasks could be made faster or less expensive? How might you imagine this happening? Certainly, a solution to a legitimate problem—such as the one addressed by License Monitor—makes compelling justification for a start-up business. But it's also good business to solve nuisance tasks, those pesky tasks that we're required to complete on a regular basis. Just as Mike Garvey of License Monitor observed an unmet need in his industry, you, too, have daily access to situations that could stand major improvement.

OPTION 3: GO FOR EFFICIENCY

Creating structure in previously fragmented (but somehow related) markets offers great potential for business ideas. By organizing the disorganized, your business makes life easier and more convenient for both product and service end users as well as for providers and suppliers. The structure and organization offered by your business also may consolidate previously disjointed markets, allowing for reduced duplication of services and costs.

Consider the case of a start-up business called RaceTown, a marketer and promoter of motor sports and related youth-oriented products and services. Its goal is "to become the largest owner, premier operator and best brand in the paved short automobile racetrack industry." RaceTown intends to capitalize on the explosive growth and popularity of NASCAR racing and similar high-energy, youth-oriented sports, including motocross, BMX racing, skateboarding, and karting. Although these sports have grown simultaneously over the past decade and have similar site infrastructure requirements, they generally operate in stand-alone facilities. RaceTown intends to colocate these sports through purchasing short oval asphalt tracks and introducing complementary services, such as restaurants, creating a chain of one-stop family entertainment facilities.

OPTION 4: SAVE THE WORLD, OR AT LEAST HELP IT OUT A BIT

The United States already has more than 1.4 million not-for-profit organizations, and approximately 47,000 new ones are created each year. The nonprofit sector employs nearly 10 percent of the U.S. workforce.[5] While starting a nonprofit organization is beyond the scope of this text, "social entrepreneurship," or developing a business that serves the needs of this ever growing market, certainly is a viable option to consider. That's exactly the approach taken by TechAction, a North Carolina–based start-up business that serves as a liaison between underemployed technology workers and nonprofit organizations needing technical support services. This start-up recognized and linked two needs with its business strategy, the first that technology workers, particularly those in career transition, need opportunities for networking and skills development to stay competitive in the job market. A logical place for them to apply these skills is in the nonprofit sector, where nonprofit organizations such as Habitat for Humanity and the United Way need technical assistance to help run their organizations more efficiently and accomplish their missions more effectively. TechAction put the two groups together, and the company now manages and bills hundreds of hours a month for technical projects for nonprofit organizations.

Another variation on a for-profit business model designed to serve not-for-profit clients is represented by Better World Books, Inc. Founded in 2002 by three University of Notre Dame students, the company has experienced growth that is nothing short of staggering—a revenue increase of more than 1,000 percent in only one year. The company collects college textbooks that are no longer wanted, resells them on Amazon and other online venues, and then channels a majority percentage of the profits into literacy support projects around the world, such as for building schools and libraries in more than twenty countries in Africa. This young company's vision is to establish book donation points at 1,000 campuses in the United States and Canada, broker 200 library book sales online, and then use proceeds to ship as many as 5 million books to Africa, endow 500 girls' scholarships in Vietnam, build twenty-five schools in India and Nepal, and fund 200 libraries in the United States.

OPTION 5: LEVERAGE KNOCKOFFS WITH A TWIST

Starbucks did not invent cappuccino, and Southwest Airlines did not invent air travel, but both companies certainly have left major marks on their respective industries. Each reversed the previous norm of its industry—Starbucks by customizing and up-pricing the cost of a cup of coffee, and Southwest Airlines by eliminating seat assignments and dropping ticket prices. In their unique ways, Starbucks and Southwest Airlines demonstrate that variations on existing business models can prove successful. The lesson here: Don't build from scratch what you can borrow or adapt.

That's essentially what eBay did when it launched an online auction company in 1995. eBay's global trading platform combined the excitement of an auction with the simplicity of a garage sale. eBay created an opportunity for virtually anyone with a computer and Internet access to market or purchase a widely diverse selection of goods and services. The upgrading of the age-old auction model eliminated the need for buyers and sellers to be colocated and created new business opportunities for millions of start-up ventures around the world.[6]

In a similar fashion, the founder of Federal Express challenged previous assumptions of the amount of time it took to transfer items from place to place. In 1965, Yale University undergraduate Frederick W. Smith wrote a term paper about the passenger route systems used by most airfreight shippers, which he viewed as economically inadequate. Smith wrote of the need for shippers to have a system designed specifically for airfreight that could accommodate time-sensitive shipments such as medicines, computer parts, and electronics.[7] The company incorporated in June 1971, began operations in 1973, and became profitable by 1975. Throughout its existence, FedEx has amassed an impressive list of firsts, most notably for leading the industry in introducing new services for customers. FedEx originated the overnight letter and was the first transportation company dedicated to overnight package delivery with guaranteed delivery times.

OPTION 6: PLAY AT WORK

Entertainment is big business. PricewaterhouseCoopers expects global entertainment and media industry spending to reach $1.4 trillion by 2007, experiencing a 4.8 percent compound annual growth rate along the way.[8] Although solutions to problems create options for new businesses, so does a sincere desire to share what you excel at and enjoy with others. Musicians, writers, and artists have acted as their own CEOs for centuries, searching out markets for their talents and skills. Avid equestrians or skiers may want to share their expertise by opening a tack shop, a sporting goods store, or perhaps even a riding stable or mountain resort. Successful companies such as LEGO and Toys "R" Us (see the mission statements for these companies later in this chapter) are two examples of highly successful businesses with a focus on fun, the former with a focus on a core product with immense popularity, and the latter as one of the world's most visible toy and game distributors.

If you want to combine work and play, one approach is to start with a unique toy, game, or skill and market it to boutique stores and niche venues that cater to nonmainstream products and services. Or start with a small storefront operation carrying niche items for targeted customers. That's what the Collins family did last year when they opened their Indiana-based skateboard business, Decks Skate Shop. Even though the local yellow pages listed five skateboard proprietors within a 20-mile radius, family members knew from their experience as consumers that only one local store actually offered a wide selection of skateboard merchandise. Sole proprietors Sandra Collins and her sixteen-year-old son Garett refurbished a former flower shop and opened their doors with a narrow but targeted merchandise line aimed at a market Garett knew well, local skateboard enthusiasts.

OPTION 7: SELL YOURSELF

Approximately sixteen million Americans are self-employed,[9] with the great majority falling into professional service skills areas. These are accountants, lawyers, physicians, dentists, and consultants, to name a few, who opt to be their own bosses rather than join larger firms. They often hire other professionals to complement their services, as well as paraprofessional office support staff. The Small Business Administration labels these entities "small businesses" until they reach the cutoff point of 500 employees. An illustration of this model is a Colorado-based start-up consortium of physicians and other medical professionals called Montrose Urgent Care (see the business plan in Appendix A). The walk-in clinic's management team recognized a void in the medical services industry of Montrose, Colorado, where only the region's emergency room was available to treat patients after hours. It also saw an opportunity for employment of local physicians seeking more flexible schedules or overtime opportunities. "Our business is a hybrid that merges the convenience of a hospital emergency room and the costs of the family practice doctor," says Mark Sawyer, Montrose Urgent Care project and business manager. "Potentially, we may also help the local hospital as it is quickly running out of space and is reluctant to expand ER Operations at this time. They're our primary 'competition' but we're moving ahead with their blessing."[10]

OPTION 8: CREATE A NEW INDUSTRY

For the true visionary, the opportunity to create not only a business but an entire industry may be the ultimate challenge. Yet even industries we take for granted today had humble beginnings. Walt Disney and his brother, Roy, spent five years getting their start-up studio off the ground before Mickey Mouse was "born" in 1928. Henry Ford and his eleven business associates launched their automobile empire with $28,000. Sam Walton opened with a single store in 1962. They, like you, began with a dream.

In tandem with these options, you'll need to give serious thought at this stage to your potential customers. Who are they? As you develop your feasibility study and business plan, you'll delve much deeper into this critical area, but because it is impossible to know too much about your customers, it's advisable to start now and think of them as often as you do your ideas for new products or services. At this stage, you need to answer the most basic of questions: Will they care about your new product or service, and why? What problem does it solve? How will your business make their lives easier, more pleasurable, less painful, or more productive? Never assume that the day you open your doors for business, the customers will automatically appear.

PUT SOMETHING ON PAPER: DEFINING YOUR MISSION, VALUES, AND GOALS

The best ideas in the world will remain little more than that if they are not put on paper and transferred into concrete objectives with deliverables and deadlines. The writing process will allow you to objectively view your business as you'll gather information to complete requirements and meet expectations for each business plan section. This task is not a linear writing assignment; you will likely find yourself jumping from section to section as the data-gathering process proceeds. Changes in one section will also trigger changes in others because competition, market share, audience preferences, financial forecasts, and product availability are all interrelated and codependent.

Three sure ways to jump-start the business plan writing process are to prepare first drafts of mission/message statements, a "blue sky" executive summary, and a logo, trademark, or other form of brand identity. Completion of these three components helps the business seem more real by providing early momentum in key business areas.

TASK 1: MISSION/MESSAGE STATEMENTS

Many business plan guides suggest beginning the writing process by developing a *mission statement,* although a mission statement is difficult to write well. A mission statement is a concise paragraph that defines a company's values, goals, and objectives. Mission statements are written to answer four basic questions: (1) why you are in business; (2) how you will succeed; (3) what your product or service is; and (4) who your customers are. Clear and compelling are the goals here, so use direct language and strong verbs in the active voice and present tense. Tom Suddes, CEO of the Columbus, Ohio–based fundraising company The Suddes Group, adds another challenge: make the message *memorable.*

"If you ask employees to stand and recite their company's mission statement, none of them can do it," says Suddes. "Yet these words are supposed to represent the company's purpose and reason for existence."[11]

Suddes counsels his clients, primarily not-for-profit organizations, to think about their message rather than their mission, by considering the impact their company has on its marketplace. "We all are bombarded with 3,000 marketing messages a day—that's over a million a year," points out Suddes. "To be successful a message has to stand out, grab my attention, and make me jump up and down."

Indeed, simplicity, brevity, and clarity are good guidelines for your entire business plan. Investors don't measure the potential for success based upon written tonnage—it's the content that counts. If you're unconvinced that less is more when it comes to preparing written documents, consider that President George Washington's inaugural speech consisted of only 134 words; the Gettysburg Address contained 276 words, and Professor Albert Einstein's theory of relativity is simplified to $E=mc^2$.

As you begin writing a draft of your mission statement, be sure to include all aspects that you consider essential: values, goals, customers, and products or services. You may need to write long passages before you can synthesize your thoughts into a short (fewer than forty words), compelling message. Some companies opt to write several mission statements, each dedicated to a core element of the business. Others include a vision statement, which redefines the future based upon the perceived impact of the new business on its industry.

Reviewing competitors' mission statements in your industry area is a good place to begin; these statements are often found on the companies' Web sites. Here are mission statements from two companies, the LEGO Group and Ben & Jerry's, to help you get started.

The LEGO mission statement:

To nurture the child in each of us.

Our mission is to nurture the child in each of us, and this means that we actively encourage self-expression through creation, thus enabling children of all ages to bring endless ideas to life.

The LEGO® experience is playing, learning, interacting, exploring, expressing, discovering, creating and imagining—all with a heavy dose of fun.

We will do this as the world leader in providing quality products and experiences that stimulate creativity, imagination, fun and learning.

This statement is accompanied by a description of the company's fundamental beliefs, the most important one being recognizing children as role models.

Children are curious, creative and imaginative. They embrace discovery and wonder, they are natural learners. These are precious qualities that should be nurtured and stimulated throughout life.

Lifelong creativity, imagination and learning are stimulated by playful activities that encourage "hands-on and minds-on" creation, fun, togetherness and the sharing of ideas.

People who are curious, creative and imaginative, i.e. people who have a childlike urge to explore and learn, are best equipped to thrive in a challenging world and be the builders of our common future.

This is what we believe and this is what our brand is building on.[12]

> ### Ben & Jerry's Mission Statement
>
> Ben & Jerry's is founded on and dedicated to a sustainable corporate concept of linked prosperity. Our mission consists of 3 interrelated parts:
>
> **Product Mission**
> To make, distribute & sell the finest quality all natural ice cream & euphoric concoctions with a continued commitment to incorporating wholesome, natural ingredients and promoting business practices that respect the Earth and the Environment.
>
> **Economic Mission**
> To operate the Company on a sustainable financial basis of profitable growth, increasing value for our stakeholders & expanding opportunities for development and career growth for our employees.
>
> **Social Mission**
> To operate the company in a way that actively recognizes the central role that business plays in society by initiating innovative ways to improve the quality of life locally, nationally & internationally.
>
> **Central to the Mission of Ben & Jerry's**
> is the belief that all three parts must thrive equally in a manner that commands deep respect for individuals in and outside the company and supports the communities of which they are a part.
>
> Source: "Ben & Jerry's Homemade Ice Cream." Retrieved from http://www.benandjerrys.com.

Corporate identities are well apparent in both the LEGO and Ben & Jerry's examples, with the statements illustrating not only markets or products, but message and meaning.

TASK 2: BLUE SKY EXECUTIVE SUMMARY

An executive summary provides a snapshot of the major components of your business. Generally less than 500 words, summaries include concise yet specific paragraphs explaining your company's history and management, product or service, industry and competition, and market(s) and financial expectations. Your mission/message statement also is included in this document, usually as an introductory paragraph. You'll also want to write a brief description of your management team, highlighting core competencies of each member.

The "blue sky" approach allows you a chance to define your best scenario for success in your summary. You will have an opportunity to examine worst-case scenarios as part of the feasibility study process—this is the time to stay positive and idealistic. Most likely you won't have enough information to complete many of the summary categories at this point, but that's acceptable at this stage. You are discovering through this process what you need to find out to eventually make each section as complete as possible. By writing an executive summary now, you can more concretely visualize the work ahead.

TASK 3: CREATE YOUR IDENTITY

You might think the easy part is naming your company. Not so. Selecting a name requires lots of research and anticipation of how you want your customers to identify your brands and services. Here's a list of important considerations to keep in mind when selecting a name for your company.

1. Is it memorable? Will your customers associate your company's name with the products or services offered? For example, many people opt to use their family name as a company name, but without a previous reputation in a given market, there may be no fixed association between your name and those products and services.

2. Is the name of your business difficult to spell or pronounce? Some family names present spelling challenges, potentially making it difficult for customers to find your business through telephone or Web directories. Pronunciation hurdles may impede the word-of-mouth factor that so many new businesses rely on for market growth, because customers may not want to share information about a company if they feel unsure about how to correctly pronounce its name.

3. Are there other businesses in your industry or geographic market that already have laid claim to the name? You'll also need to ask and answer this question as it pertains to a logo for your company and brand identification for all your products and services. In a nutshell, you need to be aware of the federal levels of protection applied to names and other identifying marks "fixed in tangible medium of expression"[13] by those who have established businesses before you. Generally speaking, trademark law protects product names, service marks, logotypes, and slogans. Copyright law protects works fixed in tangible form, such as writings, art, music, movies, and sculpture. Patent law protects inventions and the process you use to create products.

4. Is a Web domain name available that closely matches your company's proposed name? If your company's marketing and sales plans involve Internet transactions, it's essential to answer this question sooner rather than later. To do so, visit a domain registration site such as http://www.register.com and enter the potential names for your business. The site search engine will not only tell you if your desired name is taken, but also provide contact information for who owns it, allowing you the option to privately negotiate for that domain name if you wish. You also will learn what other names are available similar to the one(s) you proposed. Most businesses use a .com extension to indicate their commercial status, but .net and .biz extensions also are options.[14] Some businesses will purchase all available extensions and logical name variations at this stage to allow for redirection of Web traffic to their sites and to ensure that a future competitor won't enter the Web market using a similar domain name.

5. Does your proposed company name have visual potential? Market success is crucial for any business, but perhaps no more so than in the early stages of the company, when brand identification is being cultivated. How will the name you've selected translate to a visual identifier that your customers can instantly identify and relate to? Consider the McDonald's golden arched "M" or the blue, bold blocked "Dell," and you'll begin to recognize the impact of this relationship.

Finally, keep in mind that even the best names of businesses and their products and services are often changed as they evolve through the development process. Investors commonly rename companies as partial conditions for funding, and your feasibility study may determine that the name(s) you've selected aren't adequate to grow with the potential for your business. That's okay—business plan writing is not a linear process. Just do the best you can at this early stage, and have faith that the process outlined in the next four chapters will bring forth many of the answers sought in these preliminary stages of business development.

REVIEW

This is the time when all things are possible. But the only way a business will grow from this dream stage is for you to begin to capture your best thoughts on paper. From there, a feasibility analysis (detailed in Chapter 2) will help you determine your best approach to moving your business forward.

Five key points to remember:

1. Investors aren't sitting around waiting for you to finish your business plan. In most cases, you'll need to invest thousands of your own hours and dollars to prove your concept is viable before outside sources of funding become an option.
2. Working for yourself doesn't mean you work without experience. In fact, exactly the opposite is necessary for success. Start learning about every aspect of your business, and never stop.
3. Now is the time to think big—you can always downsize later. Trying out different options to generate a variety of ideas can only help you at this stage.
4. Low barriers to entry mean high potential for duplication. If anyone could do what you've proposed in your business idea, then why do they need you to do it for them?
5. Start today. Get your dreams for your business out of your head, and put them on paper. Write mission and vision statements, executive summaries, and slogans. Visualize as many aspects of your business as possible, and then fix them in tangible form. Only then will they begin to become real.

ASSIGNMENTS

1. There is no better time than the early stages of business plan development to create a word brainstorm list for your business. Without consideration for whether these labels apply to your company's name, brand, or mission statement, list at least fifty words that you'd like to be affiliated with your business, product, and/or service in some capacity. These can be product-specific words such as *turbo-charged* or goal-oriented words such as *triumph*. Try to avoid mundane adjectives such as *value, quality,* and *best* because their vague nature can trigger subjective interpretations. Your best choices are strong verbs and nouns that have high potential for visualization. Once you've written a master list, you can sub-categorize these words according to how they relate to your company today and where you see it evolving in the future. Ultimately, this list will provide a pool of descriptors to draw from as you write your mission statement and other preliminary documents for your company.

2. Write drafts of the mission and vision statements for your business. This is your ultimate mission and vision—not only what you hope to accomplish in the next six months (we'll tackle that challenge when we talk about milestones in Chapter 3).

3. Write a blue sky executive summary. Even if the information needed to complete this task seems highly surreal at this stage, be sure to write something related to all sections of your future business plan. Think big at this point—you're still in the anything-goes land of the hypothetical. Don't skip any key sections because you don't know how to answer them yet. Just fill in what seems right to you at this time.

4. Begin to make your business real by giving it a name and image. Review the logos and trademarks of your competition, both locally and by product or service item. A Web search is particularly useful for this assignment. Select colors and shapes that symbolize the business as you envision it. Draw key words from your word brainstorm list that epitomize what you want your business to stand for. Draft a slogan.

It is from these early decisions and roots that so much of your future business will evolve, so treat these steps with care. In revisiting LEGO Corporation, it is obvious that its brand statement of "PLAY ON"™ was the encapsulation of the LEGO® brand, its mission, values, and positioning. It is the expression of everything the brand embodies, and it speaks from the heart and soul of the brand to both external and internal audiences. It descends directly from and is closely related to the meaning of the LEGO name, literally "play well," coming from the Danish words "Leg Godt." In Latin, it means "I put together.[15] It is a perfect example of well-planted roots for a business that continues to grow more than forty years after its inception, certainly a goal worth emulating.

ENDNOTES

1. This rate is according to statistics compiled by the Small Business Administration in June 2004. "Small Business Administration." Retrieved from http://www.sba.gov.

2. Tim Sutherland, personal interview, April 8, 2004.

3. Sutherland, *supra* n.2.

4. "History." Retrieved April 25, 2005, from http://www.3m.com/about3M/history.

5. Bill Roof, "Nonprofits Growing Fast But Still a Tough Class," *Insurance Journal* online edition, November 26, 2001 (http://www.insurancejournal.com/magazines/west/2001/11/26/features/21943.htm).

6. "About eBay." Retrieved from http://pages.ebay.com/community/aboutebay/index.html.

7. "FedEx History." Retrieved from http://www.fedex.com/us/about/today/history/?link=4.

8. "Global Entertainment and Media Outlook: 2004–2008." Retrieved from http://www.pwc.com/outlook.

9. This figure is according to statistics provided by the National Association for the Self-Employed (NASE). "NASE Press Releases." Retrieved from http://news.nase.org/news/releases/2004/052004_senatebill.asp.

10. Mark Sawyer, personal interview, December 12, 2003.

11. Tom Suddes, personal interview, February 4, 2004.

12. "About us—LEGO Company—Fundamental Beliefs." Retrieved from http://www.LEGO.com/eng/info/default.asp?page=beliefs.

13. Copyright Act of 1976, Public Law 94-553, U.S. Code 17 §102(a).

14. Generally, .org extensions are reserved for not-for-profit organizations, .edu for education-related affiliations, and .gov and .mil for government- and military-related sites, respectively.

15. "LEGO.com About us—LEGO Company—The LEGO Brand." Retrieved from http://www.LEGO.com/eng/info/default.asp?page=brand.

CHAPTER

2 CAN THIS REALLY WORK?

"Get your facts first, and then you can distort 'em as much as you please."

—Mark Twain

Is your idea possible? Feasible? Practical? Now is the time to find out. It is especially important that you invest time in a solid feasibility study because its completion can save hundreds of hours later. Much of the information you gather in this phase will be incorporated into your business plan anyway, so certainly there's no wasted time on this project. Most importantly, you may realize through this process that your "great idea" is untimely, impractical, too expensive, or already someone else's business—wouldn't you prefer to know that sooner rather than later? Investing a month of work on a feasibility study can give you the confidence to move forward with your business plan or the insight to walk away before investing too much of your precious time, energy, or financial resources.

Feasibility studies consist of several distinct content areas. These areas include analyses of the industry and the company, the product and/or service, the competition, the markets you plan to enter and serve, and financial pro forma statements. Questions you need to ask and answer in each of these sections are presented in this chapter, as are suggested sequence orders for writing as well as obstacles to avoid in each section.

SECTION 1: THE INDUSTRY AND COMPANY

The objectives of this section of the feasibility study are to provide an overview of your industry and to describe the start-up and background of your company. To do this, you will need to answer the three categories of questions that follow.[1]

CATEGORY 1

What is the company's background?

    a. When and where was the company started? (Include the date and state of incorporation or partnership.)
    b. Where is the business located? Why?
    c. Have you obtained a patent or trademark for the company's name and/or logo?
    d. What is the legal structure of the company (S corporation, C corporation, or limited liability partnership)?
    e. How was your venture developed?
    f. Why did you go into business? How long did it take?

    g. What problems were encountered? How did you overcome them? What were the key milestones?

    h. Is your company affected by major economic, social, technological, environmental, or regulatory trends?

CATEGORY 2

Who are the founders and other key people involved?

    a. What skills and experiences does each member of the team bring to the business?

    b. How much money have you/they invested? How has it been used?

    c. What have been your other sources of funding?

CATEGORY 3

What industry are you in?

    a. What is the current state of the industry? How big is it in terms of total sales? Profits? Margins?

    b. Who are the major industry participants (competitors, suppliers, major customers, distributors, etc.)? What is their performance? Market share? What advantages do you have over them?

    c. What are the industry's chief characteristics?

    d. Where is the industry expected to be in five years? Ten years?

    e. Will your share increase or decrease with these changes?

    f. Who else may enter the industry?

WRITING YOUR INDUSTRY/COMPANY PROFILE

Your goal in this section is to begin to make the reader a part of your dreams. Describe how your work and decisions got the company where it is. Show how past performance will pave the way to future success. Demonstrate how you will become an important addition to the industry, and show that you understand the industry and where it is headed. You will likely need no fewer than three and no more than five single-spaced typed pages to complete this section of the feasibility study.

The following is a suggested writing sequence for the Industry/Company Profile section of your feasibility study.

Subheadings to Include
The Company
    1. Background
    2. Current Status
    3. Future Plans

The Industry
    1. Chief Characteristics
    2. The Participants
    3. Analyst Summaries
    4. Trends

THE COMPANY

BACKGROUND

This section allows you to describe the start-up and history of your company from the time of its inception. State what form of business it is and where it is located. Discuss significant milestones, such as obtaining a patent, building a prototype, signing a major contract, or obtaining trademarks on the company's name or logo. Also be sure to discuss critical people involved and the roles they have played so far.

CURRENT STATUS OF COMPANY

Discuss where you are now and how you evolved to this point. Talk about the reputation you have built, your strengths, and any limitations you are experiencing. Describe how your product is performing in the marketplace. State how much money has been invested to date, by whom, and how it has been used. If your business has any sales or service records, highlight them here. Discuss the kind and amount of funding the business needs to begin or improve operations.

FUTURE PLANS OF COMPANY

Outline your professional goals for the next three to five years. Describe how you plan to achieve them and the resources that will be needed. Be sure to allude to improvements and expansion of your existing product line as well as your hopes for increasing your market share and sales.

Outside the Box ▼

As you are writing the plan, it is important that you actually be in your business, discover the insights yourself, and let the process reveal what's missing and still in need of your attention.
—Gary Gigot, venture capitalist ▲

THE INDUSTRY

CHIEF CHARACTERISTICS OF YOUR INDUSTRY

Describe the industry your company is in by reviewing the industry's size, geographical dispersion, market, history summation, current status, and total sales and profits for each of the past three years. Discuss the competition and other players (suppliers, wholesalers, distributors, etc.) within your industry, offering a summary of each participant from weakest to strongest. Briefly discuss the participants' product/service lines and market niches. Also be sure to discuss participants with whom you will have direct involvement or competition.

ANALYST SUMMARIES OF INDUSTRY

In this section you'll need to provide a series of quotations and statements that summarize significant facts, figures, and trends about the industry from various reputable sources. Be sure you properly credit each source and provide the date of publication. Use quotations and statements from diverse sources such as industry magazines and newspaper articles. Keep in mind that quotations from personal interviews with industry leaders or analysis can also have a powerful impact. These statements should clarify where the industry is headed and the various markets to be served within the industry.

INDUSTRY TRENDS

Based on your research, you should be able to state whether your industry is declining, improving, or maintaining itself. Given your observations, discuss where you predict it might be in five to ten years and how that projection ties into your business plan. To do this, you'll need to discuss the future of the industry in terms of market need and/or acceptance and profit potential, as well as describe significant events or changes within the industry that could affect your business positively or negatively.

WHAT TO WATCH FOR

As you complete this section, you should take care to avoid several common mistakes. One mistake is including too much detail and personal opinion about the company and not enough on significant milestones and potential. Be sure to demonstrate a well-rounded knowledge of major industry players and their potential influence on the company, or you will appear to be a fly-by-night operation evidencing a lack of direction. Finally, be sure to be aware of current industry trends. Demonstrating poor or inadequate knowledge of the industry will raise doubts about the probability of your success in your new venture.

SECTION 2: YOUR PRODUCT AND/OR SERVICE

The primary objectives of this section of the feasibility study are to describe the product and related services, special features, benefits, and future development plans of your company. In three to five pages, explain what is special or different about your product and related services, and describe whom they serve. Also, you'll want to briefly highlight future plans for improvements or for introducing new products and services. To do this, you'll need to answer the following four categories of questions.

CATEGORY 1

What is the purpose of the product and/or service?

    a. Does the product solve a problem or address an opportunity?
    b. Is it a luxury item/service or a necessary item/service?
    c. How does the product/service achieve these objectives?
    d. What are its unique features (cost, design, quality, capabilities, etc.)?
    e. What is its technological life?
    f. What is its susceptibility to obsolescence? To changes in style or fashion?
    g. How does it compare with the state of the art?

CATEGORY 2

In what stage of development is the product or service?

    a. Idea
    b. Model
    c. Working prototype
    d. Small production runs
    e. Manufacturing/production
    f. Engineering prototype
    g. Production prototype

CATEGORY 3

How will the product be produced?

a. Is it capital intensive? Is it labor intensive? Is it material intensive?
b. Will all or some of the production be subcontracted? Is this an end-use item or a component of another product?
c. Is the product/service dependent on any natural, industry, or market life cycle?
d. Does your company's survival depend on someone else?
e. What new products (spin-offs) do you plan to develop to meet changing market needs, in this industry or others?
f. What liabilities might this product and/or service pose?
g. What are the insurance requirements?
h. What are the regulatory or approval requirements from government agencies or other industry participants?

CATEGORY 4

How does this product/service compare with those of competitors?

a. What kind of engineering studies, testing, and evaluation has the product undergone?
b. If more than one product is involved, how will the manufacture and/or promotion of one affect the other?
c. If equipment is involved, what is its reliability factor? What is its downtime?
d. What are the related services you will provide? How will they enhance and increase the profitability of the venture?

Following is a suggested sequence of presentation for the Product/Service section of your feasibility study.

Subheadings to Include
1. Description of Product/Service
2. Description of the Facilities
3. Proprietary Features
4. Future Development Plans
5. Product Liability

DESCRIPTION OF PRODUCT/SERVICE

Describe exactly what your product/service is, for what purpose it was designed, and what stage of development it is in. Explain in great detail how it works, special features, capabilities, and resulting benefits (economic, social, environmental, leisure, etc.). If more than one service or product is involved, discuss them and how they function together and/or affect each other.

DESCRIPTION OF THE FACILITIES

Like real estate, a major success for any business is location, location, location. Explain why you selected the one you did, referring to other businesses in the area, traffic patterns, and proximity to potential customers. If the facilities are a focus and part of the product or service (such as a hotel would be), describe them in this section. If the design of the business workspace is important to your business's success, describe what makes your facilities unique, better, or more attractive than those of your competitors, and explain why. Include costs per square foot of facilities, and state the percentage of the facilities used for revenue-producing services, operations, storage, and so on.

PROPRIETARY FEATURES

Overall, discuss how you intend to protect the integrity, confidentiality, and competitive nature of your product and service. Briefly mention any regulatory or approval requirements your product or service must meet. State who has jurisdiction and how you will satisfy these requirements. Discuss any patents, copyrights, trademarks, service marks, or other legally binding agreements that protect your product or service. State whether a patent is pending.

FUTURE DEVELOPMENT PLANS

Describe the nature and application of future development plans. Discuss whether these plans are improvements, an extension of the current product/service line, or plans for other products/services. Justify why these plans are important by showing increased or newly generated profits. State whether these plans will address your current market or other markets. Discuss the time frames for accomplishing these plans.

PRODUCT LIABILITY

Discuss the liability and insurance considerations that are inherent in manufacturing and/or marketing the product, and explain how you plan to limit this liability. Explain what type of liability insurance is necessary, and provide an estimate of the percentage of the product's cost that will be applied toward liability coverage.

WHAT TO WATCH FOR

It is extremely important that you fully describe every aspect of your product and/or service. Do not describe the product/service too technically, too broadly, or too ambiguously. Rather, focus on new, unique, or better capabilities, features, or benefits offered by your product/service. As you do this, be sure to consider the reliability, maintenance, and/or updating factors associated with your product or service. Failure to do your homework on protection availability or not showing how to protect the product/service from liability or competition is a serious oversight. Also be sure to write a strong plan for product/service improvements and expansion and how you plan to stay ahead of market needs and competition. Finally, don't forget to obtain at least one third-party evaluation of your product/service—focus group feedback or blind product trials work well here. The best scenario would be to obtain letters of intent to purchase from would-be customers.

SECTION 3: THE COMPETITION

In this section of the feasibility study you'll need to demonstrate that you are fully aware of the competitive forces at work in your marketplace. You'll also need to explain your strengths over the competition and how you will counteract their advantages and overcome or compensate for your weaknesses. Give a brief rundown on the other industry participants, highlighting your particular competitive edge along the way. You will need to answer the following four categories of questions to complete this task.

CATEGORY 1

Who are your nearest and largest major competitors?

    a. Is their business steady, increasing, or decreasing? Why?
    b. What are the similarities or dissimilarities between your business and your competitors?
    c. If you have no competition, what kind might you create by being successful in the marketplace?
    d. Do you threaten the major strategic objectives or self-image of the competition?
    e. Will you seriously affect competitors' profits?

CATEGORY 2

How does your business compare with your competitors' (strengths and weaknesses of each)?

    a. Length of time in business?
    b. Sales volume (units and dollars)?
    c. Size and number of employees, suppliers, and support personnel?
    d. Number of customers?
    e. Share of market?
    f. Product niche?

CATEGORY 3

On what basis will you compete?

    a. Product superiority
    b. Price
    c. Advertising
    d. Technology/innovation

CATEGORY 4

How is your business better?

    a. Operations
    b. Management
    c. Product
    d. Price
    e. Service
    f. Delivery

Following is a suggested writing sequence for the Competitive Analysis section of your feasibility study.

Subheadings to Include
1. Competitors' Profile
2. Product/Service Comparison
3. Market Niche and Share
4. Comparison of Strengths and Weaknesses

COMPETITORS' PROFILE

The more you know about your competition, the better. You'll need to examine both current and potential competitors in your desired marketplace based on the demographics of company size, age, locations, sales volume, management, mode of operation, and other characteristics related to similar products and services you will offer.

PRODUCT/SERVICE COMPARISON

Highlight whatever it is that makes your product/service and company more attractive in the marketplace. To do this, review similarities and differences between your product/service and that of the competition. Also be sure to compare your operations and management style with those of your various competitors.

MARKET NICHE AND SHARE

Describe where the market is headed and how each competitor's niche and share may change over the next three to five years. Discuss the competitors who have come or are coming on strong and are making (or are expected to make) bigger gains in the market. Discuss the particular segments of the market that each of your competitors addresses. State the approximate percentage each of your competitors holds in the market.

Discuss those competitors that hold the large percentages, why they have an edge, your niche in relation to them, and what percentage of the total market your niche has.

COMPARISON OF STRENGTHS AND WEAKNESSES

In this section you'll need a straightforward and honest discussion of your strengths and weaknesses in relation to your major competitors. Compare your business with others in terms of product superiority, price advantages, market advantages (large contracts with customers or suppliers; proximity to the larger market; proximity of labor supplies, raw materials, energy, transportation, land, or other resources), and management strengths and weaknesses (experience and track record, skills, etc.).

WHAT TO WATCH FOR

Certainly, you must identify all known major competitors. Do not underestimate competitive strengths and the potential of others in your industry. Be sure to demonstrate your competitive edge—what makes you different or better. Do not assume that you have no competition—this is rarely the case. That false assumption also can cause you to make two additional serious errors: (1) having no strategy for counteracting current competition or emerging competition and (2) failing to show an awareness of competitors' plans in the market and their business cycles.

SECTION 4: THE MARKET ANALYSIS

The goals of this section of the feasibility study are to demonstrate that you understand the market, that you can penetrate it, and that you are in control of the critical success factors that will enable the company to reach its sales goals. Above all, you need to prove that a market for your product/service exists and that your potential share of that market and the resulting profit projections are realistic.

Outside the Box ▼

After the fundamentals have been put in place and the content work is there, you need to focus on the design of the business. That is a set of insights—your unique approach to the market.
—Gary Gigot, venture capitalist ▲

Citing facts from your research and experiences, explain how why and how your company will be successful. After answering the following nine sections of questions, you will need seven to ten single-spaced pages to organize the material for your market analysis.

CATEGORY 1

Who or what is your target market?

a. What is the size of your target market?
b. Can this market be segmented? How (by geography, by industries, or other)?
c. Who are your customers? Are they individuals, companies, or government agencies? Are they small, mid-size, large, or global firms?

CATEGORY 2

What is the profile of your targeted customers?

a. Age
b. Gender
c. Profession
d. Income
e. Geographic location
f. Other demographics

CATEGORY 3

What are the major applications of your product or service?

a. For each major application, what are the requirements by customers?
b. What are the current ways of filling these requirements?
c. What are the buying habits of the customers?
d. What are the requirements of regulatory agencies?
e. Are your products/services bought by others to service their customers?
f. How does their industry look? How is their business doing financially?

CATEGORY 4

What is the impact (economic or otherwise) on customers who use your product or service?

a. How much will they save? What is their return on investment (benefit)?
b. Will they have to change their way of doing things?
c. Will they have to purchase other goods and services to utilize yours?
d. Will they change their work habits?
e. Overall, how will you satisfy their needs or wants better?

CATEGORY 5

What share of the market do you hope to capture?

a. What is the growth (historical and potential) of your market?
b. What are the market trends?
c. Is the market seasonal?
d. What factors will affect the market (economic, government regulation, etc.)?

CATEGORY 6

What are your market share objectives?

a. What are your market share objectives for the total available market?
b. What are your market share objectives for the service available market?
c. What are your market share objectives for the replacement market?
d. What are your rationale and costs of achieving different levels of market penetration?
e. How will you satisfy current customer needs?
f. How will you attract new customers?
g. How will you offer something new, better, or unique?
h. How will the segments and applications of your market change over the next three to five years?

CATEGORY 7

How will you distribute your product?

a. Will it be distributed under your name or someone else's?
b. Choose between direct, dealer network, wholesale, retail, or manufacturer's representative.
c. If transportation is involved, what are the implications of exporting? Importing? Taxes? Tariffs? Duties? Barriers? Foreign exchange and other concerns?

CATEGORY 8

What is the feedback from your prospective customers?

a. Have they tested a realistic prototype? How has feedback been incorporated into changes in your product/service?
b. Have you used focus groups and/or surveys to gather information from prospective customers?
c. Have you established a support/feedback system for your customers?
d. Are your service and warranty policies adequate and in keeping with regulatory requirements?

CATEGORY 9

What are your costs?

    a. What does each product/service cost you to sell?
    b. What does each product/service cost you to produce?
    c. What have (will) your profits been (be) by product/service?
    d. What are your sales figures?
    e. What are your current sales goals by product/service? Number of units?
    f. What is your sales volume in dollars?
    g. Are your sales expectations in line with the manufacturing ability to produce your product/service?
    h. Are your pricing, service, and warranty policies competitive in the marketplace?

The following is a suggested writing sequence for the Market Analysis section of your feasibility study.

Subheadings to Include
1. Target Market and Characteristics
2. Analyst Summaries
3. Market Share, Trends, and Growth Potential
4. Sales, Distribution, and Profits by Product/Service
5. Service and Warranty Policies

TARGET MARKET AND CHARACTERISTICS

Using profiles, discuss how your product/service meets the needs of your target market(s). To do this, you'll need to describe your target market(s) and explain who or what is included, especially the buying records and habits of your customers. Be certain to include pertinent facts concerning the size, age, location/area, profession, income, and other demographic information about the market. If you have conducted studies or surveys to learn about your markets, refer to them in this section and include the entire survey instrument as an appendix to your document.

ANALYST SUMMARIES

Quotations and statements should make clear what problems and needs exist in your market. It should become evident to the reader that your product/service can solve these problems and/or meet these needs better than existing methods. The objective is to pinpoint specific market opportunities that exist within the industry and how your product/service capitalizes on these opportunities. Provide a series of quotations and statements that summarize significant facts, figures, and trends about the market (and market potential) from various reputable sources. Be sure you properly credit the sources and provide the date of publication.

MARKET SHARE, TRENDS, AND GROWTH POTENTIAL

Discuss the growth potential of the entire market and your increased share. State the assumptions on which you base these growth patterns (i.e., technology development, changing customer needs, costs, etc.). Discuss your rationale and the costs and risks associated with achieving higher levels of penetration. State the percentage share of the market you have or hope to gain. Discuss the trends of the market—industrywide, regional, and local. State whether the market is seasonal, delineate the time frames, and discuss how you will adjust and compensate during the off-season. Discuss how the market may change over the next three to five years.

SALES, DISTRIBUTION, AND PROFITS

Discuss your projected sales record by product/service. State how much each product/service costs you to produce, distribute, and sell. Discuss how your product/service will be distributed and sold. Describe any unique features of your sales and distribution network.

Discuss the implications of transportation, tariffs, duties, foreign exchange, and other government regulations.

WHAT TO WATCH FOR

One of most common errors is making unrealistic market share projections (believing you can capture 100 percent of the market, or even 50 percent), as is a failure to demonstrate a clear understanding of the product or service to be sold and to which market it will be sold. For example, it is unreasonable to assume that your customer base is equally distributed throughout the markets you plan to serve. Nor can you take for granted that your primary target market represents the major portion of the demand for your product/service (the 80/20 rule—20 percent of the customers may represent 80 percent of the demand). This sometimes occurs when you address your market universally by defining it too broadly, rather than segmenting your market into various components and developing specific profiles.

Outside the Box ▼
Make sure you solve things that people actually care about. Make sure you tackle problems that are permanent and important.
—Gary Gigot, venture capitalist ▲

Another major error found in market analysis concerns sales projections and profitability expectations. These errors occur for several reasons: (1) failing to include an accurate estimate of the profitability of each product/service; (2) basing sales projections on a higher degree of output than you have adequately demonstrated can actually be met; and (3) establishing pricing that is not in line with target market needs, desires, or ability to pay.

A final critical oversight is not looking ahead in your market(s) to accurately anticipate future growth in demand for your product and/or service. This error occurs if you fail to properly assess the total market potential or changes in the market caused by economic, social, or other trends or if you fail to support target market assumptions in light of advances in technology, government regulations, population shifts, and economic forces (oil prices, interest rates, etc.)

SECTION 5: FINANCIAL FORECASTS

Without a doubt, the most difficult section of a feasibility study to write with confidence is the one concerning financial information. That's because so much of the mathematical equation is unknown or hypothetical at this early stage, so projections seem arbitrary at best. Yet without a benchmark for income, expenses, and revenue, it is difficult to move beyond the feasibility stage with the necessary confidence to build your business. One solution is to begin with the basics of start-up costs. Let's figure out what it will cost you to make what you hope to sell and then determine whether your market(s) can bear that cost.

If you plan to open your own business, you might as well also plan to spend your own money—lots of it—especially at the start-up stage. It is not uncommon for some entrepreneurs

It doesn't necessary take much capital to validate a business. Just by looking at the design you can determine if you have a niche or broad-scale product.
—Gary Gigot, venture capitalist ▲

to turn to risky options, such as obtaining cash advances from their credit cards or home equity loans, at this stage as a means of self-funding their dreams. Although small business loans from banks and personal loans from friends and family certainly are possible, you need to create the opportunity for their investment by building your business from the idea to the prototype stage. To do so, you'll need to consider and budget for five categories of start-up costs that will be required for months, maybe even years, before you open your doors for business and begin to see revenue. Be sure to include someone on your management team who has solid accounting skills, particularly if you lack this competency, because spreadsheet savvy is critical at this stage. The five categories of start-up costs are discussed next.

1. WHO YOU'LL EMPLOY

As the visionary of your business, you may be willing to forgo compensation until income is generated. However, those who work with and for you may not have the means or desire to do so. It is possible to trade future equity in the business for start-up participation at low or reduced costs, but be sure to put this agreement in writing so that all parties understand the terms of the arrangement.

Some services you'll need to either master on your own, hire for equity, or outsource. Such services and providers include legal and accounting advice and transactions and any consultants who bring needed expertise that you and your core management team lack at this point. For example, to open a restaurant, you clearly need to compensate your chef(s) and waitstaff as well as any other line service providers.

2. WHAT YOU'LL NEED TO MAKE AND SELL YOUR PRODUCT OR SERVICE

If you produce a product, you'll need to know the price of all components of that product as well as discounts and conditions applied to bulk purchases of raw materials. If you can save money by buying raw materials in bulk, you'll need to counter those savings with any additional costs required to store those materials until they are used. You'll also have production costs, which should proportionally decrease as your production volume increases. Products you create and retain for future demand are inventory, which will also incur an expense to store and manage, even though they are considered an asset. Packaging and shipping costs also are substantial and need to be carefully factored into the start-up equation.

For a service-oriented business, development costs can be easier to calculate and manage. In many cases, these costs are more arbitrary than those associated with products because they largely depend on the costs associated with your time and the time of your employees.

3. WHERE YOU'LL LIVE

Unless you plan to run your new business out of your basement or garage (the humble starting place for many successful businesses), you'll need to consider expenses for renting or purchasing an office, retail/showroom/storage space, and space to develop your product. Along with this decision comes the need to insure the property for theft, fire, or other types of losses to your property investment. Then there's the need to outfit yourself with office equipment—everything from desks to computers (with software, of course) to phones, light fixtures, and fax machines—to name just a few. If you will be transporting goods as a part of your business, you'll also need to look into some sort of reliable transportation (automobile or van) for your business.

4. WHEN YOU'LL HIT MILESTONES

The inherit passion of entrepreneurs can tempt them to want to achieve all their business goals as quickly as possible. However, fast growth of a new business can be almost as dangerous as slow growth, because your business may not be equipped to meet the demands of all its customers on an accelerated timetable. Even established businesses such as Toys "R" Us struggle with growth challenges: During its first holiday season (1998) of offering online toy purchases, the retailer was unable to keep up with high demand from Web shoppers. Consequently, many toys were not delivered by the Christmas Day deadline promised to shoppers. The following year, Toys "R" Us contracted with Amazon to handle its online toy division, resulting in a much more successful holiday retail season.

Effective management of milestones—or deadlines for reaching agreed-upon action items for your business—also is critical for successful negotiations with investors. It is not uncommon for investors to time capital infusion into businesses based upon their ability to hit milestones on or before agreed deadlines. This means that even if your contract calls for an overall investment of $500,000, you may see only percentages of that amount based upon your success in achieving stated action items. Missing just one deadline could void the overall investment contract, so it is essential to be cautious when assessing a timetable for growth. For example, rather than agreeing to sell a certain number of units by April 15, write the milestone with a completion date of the second fiscal quarter—thereby providing a few extra months of time to account for miscalculations or overly optimistic expectations.

Milestone management also includes a serious appraisal of inventory management. For service organizations this is a relatively easy task, assuming that you know—unequivocally—that the required labor is available when and where you need it. A product-based business needs to tread more carefully here. Key questions are what will the demand for your product(s) be once it hits the shelves? How quickly can you develop new product to replace what is sold? What components are required to create your product, and how quickly can you acquire them from your suppliers? How much inventory should you keep readily available, and how much can you develop using the just-in-time model? The answers to these questions certainly impact your start-up costs because funds invested in producing inventory are obviously not available for other necessities, such as marketing or administrative costs.

5. HOW YOU'LL MARKET YOUR BUSINESS

From business cards to shrink wrap, you'll need to consider how you present your business to the world. These costs add up quickly and are frequently the ones underestimated by new business owners. Besides business cards, you may need letterhead stationery, brochures, or other written material explaining the features and benefits for your product/service, as well as directions for appropriate use. Packing and shipping costs also can be overlooked—will you use boxes and mailing labels bearing your company name and logo? You will also need to spend money to promote your business through advertising, with costs that vary widely. A single newspaper ad might cost $250 to $300, whereas a television commercial could cost between ten and a hundred times that amount. A simple listing in the local telephone directory costs several hundred dollars per year. A company Web site will require initial investment of several thousand dollars to get up and running and then additional monthly maintenance fees. From billboards to radio spots and flyers to storefront signs, getting the name of your business into the marketplace requires a considerable up-front investment.

Outside the Box ▼

Very often, the best business opportunities occur when everyone else has turned their head away from a needed solution.
—Gary Gigot, venture capitalist ▲

SECTION 6: MANAGEMENT TEAM

Your team is the heart and soul of your business—its members will implement the plan you are working so hard right now to develop. The old advice to "surround yourself with the smartest people you can find" definitely applies to start-ups. You are investing considerable time and energy to launch your business; expect nothing less of those who work with and for you. It is important to have business core competency skills close at hand in addition to those skills necessary to run any successful business (such as financial acumen and technical expertise). An honest assessment of skills in hand versus skills needed versus optimal skills desired is appropriate here, allowing you to develop a gap analysis of what your team has versus what it needs. One approach to bridging these gaps is to develop an advisory board for your business. This group consists of individuals selected for their expertise, experience, and insight in narrow but critical business spectrums. Physicians, college professors, engineers, scientists, or even fashion designers are potential advisory board candidates—let the nature of your business be your guide. Include biographical sketches of your advisory board in the Management Team section of the business plan. You also will want to include summarized professional biographies in this section as well as complete resumes as an appendix to this section.

Interview with Venture Capitalist Gary Gigot

Gary Gigot is a general partner with Frazier Technology Ventures, a seasoned marketing executive, and an active private investor in the Puget Sound area. Gigot has been instrumental in deal analysis, portfolio development, and fund strategy with FTV. His technology experience includes serving as vice president of marketing at Microsoft Corporation from 1990 to 1994, where he managed the advertising, public relations, research, channel, events, and direct marketing disciplines. From 1994 to 1999, Gigot was both an investor in Visio

continued

Corporation and its chief marketing officer, where he played a central role in positioning Visio as the leader in business drawing software. During his Visio years, the market capitalization rose from $25 million to $1.3 billion, after which the company was sold to Microsoft. Gigot remains an active philanthropist, having founded the Gigot Center of Entrepreneurial Studies at Notre Dame and the United Way of King County's "Out of the Rain" initiative to end homelessness. Mr. Gigot sits on the Mendoza College of Business Advisory Council.

"The business planning process is generally well understood, and there are books and software that can help an entrepreneur in creating the plan that develops a business idea. What I have found after having reviewed hundreds of plans in either narrative or PowerPoint format is that there are two embedded elements in these plans that generally make the winners stand out from the losers.

"The first is simple: Does the entrepreneur have a good idea? I've seen plans for everything from game board companies to mall kiosks to local car racing parks to wireless services to horticulture companies to printed displays to Web services to enterprise software companies. No matter what segment the business is in, you are always looking to assess and judge the quality of the idea.

"The second element that is closely related is what I've come to call the *design of the business*. In each investing area, the key design factors will be different, but through all the pages of analysis and writing, you have to see four to six key design factors that give the business the best chance for scaled growth, embedded profitability, competitive advantage, and, thus, systematic investor return.

"In our venture firm we generally describe these design points in an investment thesis. In angel networks, they likely need to emerge in the fifteen-minute PowerPoint presentation. But you must be able to create design factors in your business that create unique advantages, points of leverage, high margin opportunities; open large, untapped markets; and take a quality idea or innovation and turn it into a successful enterprise."[2]

REVIEW

Five key points to remember are these:

1. A thorough feasibility study is a lot of work, but its completion enables you to move to the next stage of business plan development with confidence. Exactly like it takes money to make money, it takes time to figure out whether additional time invested in your new venture is well spent. Don't skimp on time in this tremendously valuable process.

2. A feasibility study is an internal document, an accumulation of information and data that will give you insights needed to take the next steps in developing your business. It will not be read by external audiences, so don't spend time polishing its prose. The writing process certainly helps in idea formulation, however, so don't skip this part entirely. The business plan is where you'll want to invest your efforts in a well-written and attractively presented document.

3. Do not feel frustrated if you seem to have more questions than answers within the major sections of your feasibility study, especially the financial section. That's quite normal at this point. You are actually learning what you'll need to know, which is much better than forging ahead without a map into unknown territory. The process of asking tough questions about your potential market and competition works as a trigger, enhancing your ability to uncover information in these areas.

4. Product businesses generally cost more to start than service businesses but also provide more barriers to entry against would-be competitors. However, "bootstrapping" is much easier for service than product businesses because the service is marketed based on the skills of the entrepreneur/employees rather than the successful development of product prototypes. Either way, you'll need to pay close attention to your start-up costs to be sure you'll have enough financial resources to actually get the product or service to market.

5. If you don't have expertise in needed areas, develop an advisory board and "borrow" that expertise to help get your business off the ground. Surround yourself with intelligent and experienced people by compensating them with an equity stake in the business (as well as a salary if you can afford it). Even though you are the business visionary, you'll need a strong team around you to build your business.

ASSIGNMENTS

1. Using the approach outlined in this chapter, research and compile information as it pertains to each major section of your feasibility study. This information includes the following:
   a. Company and industry
   b. Product and service
   c. Competitive analysis
   d. Market analysis
   e. Financial analysis

2. Develop a list of names of individuals who you think would be assets on an advisory board for your business. Be sure to select individuals who have unique expertise and with whom you feel comfortable sharing proprietary company information.

3. Be sure your resume is up to date, as well as those of all members of your management team. Be sure to highlight skills from past employment that you plan to emphasize in your new business venture.

As you complete what will likely seem a mountain of work in this process, take heart that most of what you are working on is directly transferable into the business plan. That challenge awaits you and is presented in Chapter 3.

ENDNOTES

1. Feasibility material developed in collaboration with Professor Jeff Bernel, University of Notre Dame. Used with permission.
2. Gary Gigot, personal interview, April 28, 2004.

CHAPTER

3 ROLL UP YOUR SLEEVES AND START WRITING

"What is written without effort is in general read without pleasure."

—Samuel Johnson

If you've done the hard work of Chapter 2, completing your feasibility study, the next step in the development of your business should be much easier than you might expect. It's time to write your business plan. A business plan is not a novel, but it needs to be compelling and believable. Nor is it a term paper, but it needs to be precise, factual, and well documented. The business plan is a living document in that it will never really be completed. Rather, it will be a work in progress, evolve with your business, and adapt to incorporate the feedback of others who read it. But for now, it is a composite of the data mining you accomplished during the feasibility study phase. If you've thoroughly completed the assignments of Chapter 2, much of your business plan content should be in hand. The challenge now is to use that content to build a compelling story in support of your business idea and plan for implementation.

Despite expectations for inclusion of at least ten different types of data and information, most experts agree that your plan should not exceed twenty to twenty-five pages. It should be neatly prepared with logical section headings, single-spaced type no larger than 12-point type and no smaller than 10-point type, and in an easily readable font such as Times Roman. It will make liberal use of bulleted points and tables to display pertinent data. Of course, your plan will also include a cover page, table of contents, page numbers, and all necessary citations.

Following are the major section headings for a typical business plan, although it is important to note that the order in which they appear is not the order in which you need to write them. We will spend the remainder of this chapter discussing each major section in detail. Feel free to jump into writing whatever section is most appealing to you or the section for which you have the greatest amount of information available. Business plan development is anything but a linear process.

MAJOR BUSINESS PLAN COMPONENTS

- Executive Summary
- Description of Company
- Description of Industry
- Description of Product or Service
- Competitive Analysis

- Market Analysis
- Marketing Plan (sales and promotion strategies)
- Management Team
- Financial Analysis
- Appendices

EXECUTIVE SUMMARY

If you completed your Chapter 1 homework, you've already written a blue sky executive summary. That's your ideal outcome to this process, a description of your business if all goes right, if milestones are completed on time, and if market expectations turn out to be realistic or even favorable. That's a lot of "ifs." If that's actually happened to you, congratulations—you are definitely in the minority of start-up businesses. But the real purpose of the blue sky summary was only to get you thinking about how you'd like to see your business materialize if you could—a "crystal ball" version. In actuality, your final executive summary really should be a highly condensed version of your business plan.

Even though the executive summary appears first in the business plan, many entrepreneurs find it easier to write last, after they have completed their plans. That's because a good summary will concisely offer highlights of each section of your plan, with the exception of the appendices. Obviously, it is difficult to write highlights if you haven't worked out the details. You'll want to strike a balance here—offering enough description so that the reader can read only the executive summary and understand the key aspects of your business but not so much that it exceeds two pages of single-spaced text. See Appendix A for an example of an executive summary written for start-up health care facility Montrose Urgent Care.

DESCRIPTION OF THE COMPANY

The description of the company is the section of the plan where you describe the decisions you have made about the formation of your company and other pertinent facts regarding its history and development. You'll need to include the company's name and address, legal status (sole proprietorship, limited liability corporation, or partnership), date of formation, and brief description of your business and industry type, along with a product/service overview. If you haven't made some of those decisions, it is acceptable to discuss your intentions using the future tense. Any significant milestones, such as developing a product prototype, testing your product with focus groups, or generating sales and profits, should be briefly mentioned here as well. If you have written a mission or vision statement, you also want to include them in this section.

DESCRIPTION OF INDUSTRY

It's easy for entrepreneurs to become consumed with their businesses and overlook the industries within which the businesses exist. Yet no business will succeed in a vacuum, and your business will undoubtedly be affected by trends within your industry. Better to understand and plan for those realities at this stage than be caught off guard by them later. Through your feasibility analysis work you've gathered much of the information you will need for this section. Let's begin with answering six basic questions.

1. What life stage is your industry in? Is it a blank slate with lots of start-up companies, more mature but with room for growth, or a longtime, established presence with leaders in market share clearly defined?

2. Related but not identical to an industry life stage is its growth rate. An immature industry may grow quickly but fizzle out almost as fast—the rapid ascent and then demise of numerous dot-coms is only one example of this. Concurrently, an over-the-hill industry might grow by only 1 percent each year, well below national averages representing the growth of the national economy. Declining industries may show ongoing losses in market share as a result of foreign competition.

3. How much competition is in your industry, how fast are the competitors growing, and what is fueling that growth? Based upon the industry's life stage and growth rates, how likely is it that more competition will enter the industry over the next twelve to thirty-six months?

4. Are you in more than one industry? For example, a bakery franchise that specializes in diabetic and sugar-free products is in both the food and health industries.

5. Is this industry seasonal? If so, are there off-season opportunities to generate revenue? Some ski areas, for example, have turned their slopes into summer recreation areas. And some sports teams have opened their stadium facilities for conferences and concerts.

6. What are the barriers to entering this industry? While costs are a common barrier, other significant factors include government regulations or licensing requirements, product testing, or safety inspections, to name a few. Does your business meet these required criteria?

DESCRIPTION OF PRODUCT OR SERVICE

As discussed in Chapter 2, it is essential to include in your business plan a thorough description of how your product/service was developed, how it currently works, and in what capacities and at which milestones it will evolve. All components of the product or service need to be detailed here, as do the sources for those components. Lists of specific attributes of products and services work well here, with special emphasis on those features you consider to be proprietary. Inventory requirements and demands are also appropriate to include in this section. When possible, use visuals to show readers what a product looks like; this is especially important if you've developed or tested a prototype. You also will want to begin to explain how your product/service differs from that currently in the marketplace. There's no need for elaborate detail on this aspect, however, as that information typically presents itself in the marketing plan section of your document.

COMPETITIVE ANALYSIS

If you remember only one thing about competition, remember that you always have it, even if it isn't apparently obvious. The statement "We have no real competition" only serves to identify you as an amateur, so just don't say it. Don't even think it, because it is simply not true. Even if no other business is serving the geographic base of your defined market, the realities of e-commerce enable customers to shop online vendors with convenience and ease. And there's always competition for the disposable-income dollar—if your customers do not purchase your product/service, how else will they spend their money?

Probably the most important outcome of the competitive analysis section is to show the reader which other companies share the same market space as you propose to serve and how successful they have been in their efforts to date. As you do this, keep in mind that not all competition is created equal—differentiations in product/service quality, availability, and price play major roles here. Besides looking at existing competition, be sure to think about who else could enter your target market(s) and what it would take to do so. In general, service-related businesses tend to have lower barriers to entry, making them easier to replicate than product-related businesses. Internet-based businesses also are easier to get up and running than brick-and-mortar ones. Be honest about your competition, and be thorough in evaluating its strengths and weaknesses in comparison with your own. But don't be discouraged—a market with no competition offers no opportunity. In the unlikely event that you find yourself in such a market, ask whether your business is premature, obsolete, or not something that customers want or need.

MARKET ANALYSIS

Do you really know who your customers are? For the sake of your future business, the answer had better be yes. You should have collected demographic information for potential customers during the feasibility analysis stage. In addition to offering valuable insight into what makes your customers purchase one product or service over another, the market analysis also is essential information in the development of your marketing plan. One major error in this section is ambiguity. Defining market boundaries doesn't limit potential customers; it only makes developing a plan to reach them much more manageable. Too generic a market (for instance, all residents over the age of forty-five who live in Peoria, Illinois) may falsely convey a market size that is larger than realistic. Besides basic demographic information of age, gender, income, marital status, occupation, level of education, ethnic heritage, family size, and home ownership status, you'll need to gather geographic specifics of an urban, rural, or suburban residency and the corresponding characteristics of those neighborhoods.

Another category of critical information is the understanding of how your target markets think about and spend money. What are their priorities? Priorities are largely tied to lifestyle choices, which in many (but not all) cases are tied to age. Teenagers tend to spend money on clothes, CDs, DVDs, and other items for personal use, and working adults with homes likely spend more time in Home Depot. Delving deeper, you can learn by gathering psychographic data how factors such as fear, self-esteem, and social status impact the purchasing decisions of your target market. In short, it is all but impossible to know too much about your potential customers.

MARKETING PLAN

The marketing plan section is where you take all the data you've gathered about your target market(s) and put them to work. You need to develop a sales strategy, including the best way to reach your customers, what to tell and show them about your product/service, how to get them to remember your product/service, and how to convince them to purchase your product/service on a continued basis. Low price points alone do not guarantee sales; if they did, subcompact car sales would regularly outpace SUV or luxury models, and Tiffany's would have gone out of business long ago.

Breaking down the sales process into three definable categories is a good starting point. These categories are presale, point-of-sale, and postsale.

1. PRESALE: REACHING YOUR CUSTOMERS AND TEACHING THEM ABOUT YOUR PRODUCT

From the McDonald's golden arches to the Goodyear blimp, product identification is a core component of a business identity and reputation. Through targeted advertising, you'll promote these shorthand versions of the company's mission, niche, and reason for existence to potential customers. It is important to select advertising outlets where your customers already are congregated—few people go looking for marketing messages. Options include advertising in newspapers, magazines, or trade journals; on radio and/or television; via Internet; or with brochures, posters, flyers, or billboards. Don't forget to list your business in the local telephone directory. Besides the visual identification of your product, service, and business and their distinctive features, your marketing message should convey basic information such as price, features, and purchase location options.

2. POINT OF SALE: SELECTING YOUR PRODUCT/SERVICE OVER ALL OTHERS

Whoever said that "you can't judge a book by its cover" hadn't given much thought to consumer behavior. Very often, the "cover" or packaging of a product yields great influence on the decision to purchase one item rather than another. How your product/service is presented certainly will factor into the customer's decision to buy it, so be sure you give this marketing element considerable attention. Service items may not require as much packaging as product items, but it is advisable to offer a brochure or another written document explaining your policies, procedures, expectations for payments, and service guarantees.

All products should be tastefully and professionally packaged in a secure fashion to avoid tampering. The product cover should convey enough information for the consumer to make comparisons with alternate products, as well as price and other inventory data (retailers may take responsibility for some of these requirements). If supplemental products such as batteries are required to make your product work correctly, be sure that information is clearly displayed. Internal packaging such as brochures or fact sheets should include instructions for assembly and use, warranty/guarantee information, and company contact information should questions arise. Yes, you need to design and write all this material or hire a public relations firm to help you. Be sure to field test all marketing materials to determine whether the results match those you were seeking.

You also need to give serious thought to the manner in which you would like your product or service to be sold. Thinking that you can do everything yourself is shortsighted; you're going to need some help. But with help comes training and compensation, which also require a bit of brainstorming. You also need to justify salaries for sales employees based upon reasonable expectations for your sales. Think about the role the salesperson plays in the decision process of your customers—will they need lots of help in understanding the product or service, or is it more or less self-explanatory? Does the product require a showroom environment to generate sales, or could it virtually sell itself on the Internet? Are telephone or mail-order sales an option, or will your products/services be sold through third-party retail outlets? You'll need answers to all these questions before making salesforce hiring decisions.

3. POSTSALE: A REPEAT CUSTOMER IS (USUALLY) A HAPPY CUSTOMER

Unless your business holds a monopoly on a product/service that is perceived as critical, there is absolutely no guarantee of customers, never mind repeat customers. Yet they are the lifeblood of a business that survives the start-up stage to expand and move into stability. How can you ensure that your customers come back? Some important factors include the following:

1. Knowing who they are, via product or service registration or another means allowing for follow-up communication
2. Continued communication via e-mail, direct mail, or other means announcing your business's new products and services
3. Sending or providing samples of other related products and services to existing customers
4. Inviting existing and potential customers to open house events at your business
5. Developing and maintaining a company website so that new and existing customers can obtain additional product/service information with ease

Probably the most important postsale activity is one that you have little influence over but certainly could suggest to your customers. The tried-and-true "word of mouth" response to sales is most trusted and often used; making it essential that your customers have only good things to say to their friends about your business, products, and services.

MANAGEMENT TEAM

In all likelihood, you're reading this book because you have a great idea that you want to turn into a great business. That makes you the founder of your company. Congratulations—you've made it to the top. But just as a roof can't exist without a foundation, your business will be hard pressed to move forward without other key personnel. At a minimum, you'll need to surround yourself with people who possess core skills in each critical component of your business: marketing and sales, accounting, product and service research and development, human resources, legal, and technology, to name only a few major categories. Include a resume for each key personnel member in an appendix of your business plan, and be sure these resumes highlight skills for which each member is accountable in your business. Be sure to summarize key skills of each team member in the management section, however, because not all investors read appendices.

Knowing your strengths and weaknesses is essential here—are you a big-picture visionary with little patience for details? If so, you'd better have a staff to fill those gaps if you wish to be successful. If you've not already done so, consider taking the Myers-Briggs Personality Test to determine your professional strengths and weaknesses. Shore up your self-proclaimed weaknesses with the skills of others who report themselves strong in your weaker areas.

Tim Sutherland, CEO of Pace Global Energy Services of Fairfax, Virginia, has learned first-hand the importance of hiring the right people for the right positions. He explains: "The most important thing of the organization is to make sure the leadership exudes a common personality and a willingness to be adaptive to the market and to each other. Consistent values, dependability, are what you care about. There is no salary structure that will replace a sense of comfort that is derived from that. If there is a dichotomy, it can fracture the organization.

"The secret is to make sure that senior management exude the right message. Take care in hiring. When we hire someone, everyone from the receptionist to the vice presidents interview—it's a hire from all over the company at all levels. It's a cake testing process," says Sutherland.[1]

One way to augment your team's credentials is to add the skills and experience of an advisory board. This board comprises individuals who have high levels of experience and success in narrow but relevant areas to your business, products, and services. Their role is similar to that of consultants as you develop and launch your business. They also are a good source of contacts to funding leads as well as assistance on other essential matters. An advisory board differs from a board of directors in that the advisory board has no legal accountability to the company, and vice versa, and its members likely have invested time but not money in the start-up stage. Conversely, board of director members often have contributed financially to the company. During the early stages of the business, the Board of Directors may be made up of founding/key personnel. Once outside funds are accepted from angel investors or venture capitalists, the board demographics typically change to reflect these outside interests.

Another key objective of the management team section is to discuss how your business will be run day in and day out. This includes who reports to whom, key personnel responsibilities, supervisory functions and roles, and expectations for communication within the organization. One of the most complicated aspects of building structure in a start-up business is salary: How much will you pay yourself and those who work for you? While it may be tempting to redirect all funds back into the

Outside the Box ▼

"The most important thing of the organization is to make sure the leadership exudes a common personality, and a willingness to be adaptive to the market and to each other."

—Tim Sutherland, CEO, Pace Global Energy Services ▲

business, the practical matter of how to support yourself is an ever-present conundrum. If you work elsewhere, you'll have alternate income but much less time to devote to your business. Your staff, while supportive, may not be in a financial position to forgo salary (even if they take an equity stake, stock, or stock options in the business, it still won't buy this week's groceries). Your example is important here—do not ask others to sacrifice for your business what you are not also willing to do without.

An additional element that can appear in the management team section of the business plan is milestones. However, because these deadlines for deliverables are commonly tied to financial objectives, you may opt to include them in that section instead. The logic for including them in the management team section is that milestones are directly tied to decisions made by key management personnel. What's certain is that without effective management, milestones are likely to go unmet. That's bad news if you're anticipating investment funding, as many venture capitalists make funding phases contractual and conditional upon reaching agreed-upon milestones within predetermined deadlines. Just one slipup from a team member could negate an entire contract and put future funding for your business in serious jeopardy.

Outside the Box ▼

"I look for a captivating idea with growth potential, a sustainable competitive advantage, a strong and experienced team, a logical go-to-market strategy, and a sound financial plan."
—Dave Brenner, Managing Partner, IdeaWorks ▲

FINANCIAL ANALYSIS

Although this section rarely appears first in business plans, it is often the section that potential investors first turn to when reading your document. In its simplest form, this section depicts where and how you spend money and how much you expect to earn as a result of doing so. Generally spanning three to five years in time, the data is broken down by month for the first year and quarterly thereafter. If you opt for a five-year forecast, it is generally acceptable to supply annual data for years four and five because the number of unknowns that impact start-ups tend to jeopardize the credibility of long-term financial projections.

The financial analysis section will include an income statement, balance sheets, cash flow statements, a summary of assumptions, a break-even analysis, and a description of the funding request and proposed use of funds. Start-up businesses lacking historical financial data will complete this section pro forma or by projecting expected financials into the future. Specifics of each section are described next.

1. *Income statements* simply show whether your company is making or losing money, which explains why this is also sometimes called a profit-and-loss statement. As part of this formula, income statements also show the distinction between gross profits (revenues less costs), labor and expense costs, and pre-/posttax net income.
2. *Balance sheets* offer a record of a company's wealth in terms of its assets and liabilities. Assets are divided according to the type of items owned by the business (furniture, for example, is a fixed asset, as is land, computers, or buildings); owed to the business (accounts receivable); and cash, inventory, and any expenses you already have prepaid (current assets). Liabilities are what you owe as a business, including payroll and taxes, bills yet to be paid, and any long-term debt such as a lease payment. What's left over

when you subtract liabilities from assets is net worth (let's hope this is a positive number) or equity, which gets added back into the balance sheet so that both sides match and add up to the same number.

3. *Cash flow statements* show how much cash is available to the business at any given time, yet they are calculated on a monthly and/or quarterly basis. That's not to say that cash isn't looked at very closely between reporting periods—some start-ups monitor their cash daily, if not weekly. To calculate cash flow, subtract all fixed expenses (such as rent and salaries) from available cash, and then subtract expenses that could be considered variable (advertising, office supplies). Be sure to take into account deadlines for your expenses. Your cash flow is the difference between what you have and what you spend each month. Sounds easy enough, but the challenge is figuring out how much cash will come from which sources, and when. One obvious but not always easy projection is cash sales. If you do not have a history of sales because your company is in the infancy stage, it's best to be extremely conservative here. Clearly, it's better to have more cash than you expected than less cash than you need. Also include cash that may come in the form of loans or loan repayments to you, as well as any credit-based funds available for use.

Successful entrepreneurs emphasize the need for accuracy in cash flow statements because mistakes here can lead to serious problems, including bankruptcy. Pace Global Energy Services CEO Tim Sutherland still watches cash flow at his multi-million dollar energy company as closely as he did when he founded the business twenty-five years ago. "It's the most important thing we monitor. We monitor cash flow more than any other metric," says Sutherland. "Absent continued outside funding, cash flow and working capital drive the business."

Stable companies such as Sutherland's use cash flow analysis for all major business decisions. He explains that "in a business like this, there are always new opportunities to entertain. Irrespective of how lucrative an opportunity appears, the first thing we look at is 'is this an opportunity we can afford to fail at.'

"The distance between the description of an opportunity on day one and the pot of gold at the end is two times longer, and the pot of gold always seems smaller than originally envisioned," adds Sutherland. "We plan for that to happen and see if we can afford the failure of this opportunity. We look at cash flow and access to capital throughout the entire continuum."

4. *Assumptions* are directly tied to the decisions that you are making in calculating your financial projections. They are the rationale for why you are projecting *growth* for your company and under what circumstances. How fast will your company grow? How quickly will you obtain target market share? How many people will you hire in what positions, and why? It's not enough to simply list dates and deadlines—you need to explain why you believe as you do and show any evidence that exists to help others draw similar conclusions. Throughout this process, you should be true to your core competency as a business, cautions Sutherland, or you might make decisions that could harm rather than help growth in the long run.

After cash flow, growth is the indicator most critical to Sutherland, and it is ever-present in his assumptions, particularly as they pertain to strategic partnerships. "You need to have a good sense what the business will look like with and without growth," he explains. "But remember that growth in and of itself is not the goal; sustained profitability is the goal.

"Look at the growth opportunities that are available with the realization that some are not a match for your core competency," he continues. "Access the expected value of the growth opportunity on its merits and how it relates to core competencies of your organization. The lack of alignment that fragmentation causes is very costly."

5. *Break-even analyses* calculate, as the name suggests, the point at which the amount of money you've invested in your business is equal to the amount of money that you've earned. That's not to say that you are yet profitable, but you are no longer losing money trying to cover your monthly fixed and variable expenses. To determine this figure, divide your monthly fixed expenses by your gross profit margin (which will take into account variable costs because they are subtracted from your gross cost of goods). Under some circumstances, you may wish to include this information in your "Assumptions" section, noted earlier.

6. *Funding request/use statements* explain how much money you have received from investors and lenders and what, in turn, you have promised to them (such as an equity stake in the company and/or stock options). Disclosure is important here—do not be tempted to "forget" to include loans from friends and family if they come with expectations for repayment or other conditions. If you have assigned a value to your company, it is appropriate to include that valuation in this section (but be prepared to have it disputed by investors!).

This section also outlines how you will use additional funds if they are obtained. Common uses are the expansion of staff and/or salesforce, purchase of necessary equipment or inventory, expansion of the business into new geographic, product, or service areas, and increased marketing. (Note: Investors generally do not want to see their funds used to pay down preexisting debt).

Outside the Box ▼

"Growth in and of itself is not the goal; sustained profitability is the goal."
—Tim Sutherland, CEO,
Pace Global Energy Services ▲

When you complete the financial analysis section, be sure to have an accountant or a likewise-trained financial professional review it for completeness and accuracy. You'll also want to regularly review this section—factors outside your control (such as shifts in the local economy) can impact pro forma statements.

APPENDICES

Appendices are not mandatory to your plan, but most entrepreneurs include them. Limiting the main business plan to twenty-five pages is a good idea because information overload can discourage some readers from reviewing your plan. However, you may have supplemental information you wish to share; if you do, this is the place to share it. Material commonly found in appendices includes diagrams and/or photos of products/services; letters of endorsement, resumes of key personnel, letters of intent from potential customers, results of customer surveys, a SWOT (*s*trengths, *w*eaknesses, *o*pportunities, and *t*hreats) analysis, details of manufacturing or technology contracts related to your business, organizational charts, or other contractual details too intrinsic for inclusion in the main document.

WHAT TO WATCH FOR

IdeaWorks managing partner Dave Brenner reads a lot of business plans, often more than 500 per year. In his thirty years of advising start-up ventures, he's learned firsthand what works and what doesn't. He offers the following advice:

The best business plans will offer a clear linkage between the entrepreneur's vision and operating milestones. I look for a captivating idea with growth potential, a sustainable competitive advantage, a strong and experienced team, a logical go-to-market strategy, and a sound financial plan.

Most importantly, I want clear permission to believe in the business. Does the pitch or plan reflect an idea that might work or must work?[2]

So what sends up red flags for Brenner? Here is a list of typical pitfalls.

- Inarticulate expression of the core idea
- Gross oversimplification of the issues
- No credible go-to-market strategy
- Overstating market share potential
- The lack of team composition and relevant experience
- Ambiguous sources and uses of funds
- An unclear role for the investor

Gary Gigot of Frazier Technologies summarizes with another perspective. "It doesn't necessarily take much capital to validate a business," he says. "Just by looking at the design you can determine if you have a niche or broad-scale product.

"As you are writing the plan, it is important that you actually be in your business, discover the insights yourself, and let the process reveal what's missing and still in need of your attention," concludes Gigot. "Think about not just what your business is, but what it could become."[3]

REVIEW

This chapter breaks writing tasks associated with your business plan into distinct and manageable sections. These sections include the Executive Summary, Description of Company, Description of Industry, Description of Product/Service, Competitive Analysis, Market Analysis, Marketing Plan, Management Team, Financial Analysis, and Appendices. Do not be overwhelmed by writing an entire plan. Simply take one section at a time. Write in any order that feels comfortable to you, but rearrange sections to reflect the order described here prior to submitting your plan for review by investors and other audience groups. Keep in mind that business plans are "living documents" in that they are never really completed. Rather, they offer a road map for your business's development and growth. You'll want to revisit your business plan at least annually to see how your business achievements measure up to your projections.

ASSIGNMENTS

1. Begin setting short- and long-term goals for your business. Working backward, identify the goals you would like your business to achieve at months 36, 24, 12, and 6. Then make a list of what you need to accomplish to make each of these goals a reality. These are your action items.

2. Conduct a gap analysis of the skills possessed by your management team. Where is there overlap or deficiency? What are your team's strengths and weaknesses? Generate a list of potential advisory board members based on desired skills and perceived weaknesses. This group can help fill those gaps until you have adequate funding to staff additional positions.

3. If you can gain access to other business plans, review them as potential models for your own. Although no two plans are the same, ideas for organizing content or useful appendix material are often transferable.

4. Taking each section in turn, write your business plan. When you have a draft that feels comfortable, share it with all members of your team as well as your advisory board, and ask for constructive feedback.

5. Challenge your plan by testing it for readability and completeness. One way to determine whether your plan is reader friendly is to read it aloud. If your plan's sentence structure mimics the natural pauses and breaks in speech, you're probably on the right track. If you're unable to read your sentences without gasping for breath, or if they sound stilted or awkward, you've likely written sentences that are too long, composed in the passive voice, or have too much extraneous information. Even with business plan writing, simple often works best.

ENDNOTES

1. Tim Sutherland, personal interview.
2. Dave Brenner, personal interview.
3. Gary Gigot, personal interview.

CHAPTER

4   SHOW YOUR PLAN TO THE WORLD

"First learn the meaning of what you say, and then speak."

—Epictetus

Some of us begin honing our presentation skills in kindergarten. That's often when we're introduced to the longtime classroom tradition of "show and tell," a chance to bring a favorite toy to school and talk about it in front of other children. Many teachers also allow for a Q-&-A session with the audience, giving children early opportunities to experience planned versus spontaneous commentary.

Good business plan presentations are a lot like "show and tell" in that they offer the opportunity to verbalize and demonstrate concepts that previously may have been limited to written descriptions. Learning retention research shows that audiences are 75 percent more likely to remember information if it is presented in a visual, aural, and written format simultaneously rather than in only one medium.[1] As a document author, you also face a challenge in determining what information to keep or eliminate as you move from a document that supports written communication toward spoken communication.

Audience analysis is critical to the development of any successful presentation plan. That is no different in the presentation of a business plan than it would be in any other speaking opportunity. It is critical to understand audience group demographics and dynamics so that you can effectively anticipate people's questions, concerns, and likely reactions to your business idea. So what types of audience groups are you likely to encounter? Here's a typical, but not exhaustive, list.

1. Investors. Be they accredited venture capitalists or your second cousin twice removed, investors are central to the process of building new businesses. Yet that is where the similarities end. Venture capitalists frequently consolidate resources in funds or firms and often are professionally managed and industry specific (investing only in technology-related or minority-owned firms, for example). They and angel investors (high-net-worth private individuals) will see your business in terms of its ability to grow quickly, be profitable, and build market share. Your friends and family may be more attuned to your dream of building your own business and are good sources for the start-up capital needed to get the business off the ground. With even the best written business plan, investors aren't interested in supporting good ideas. You'll need a prototype and some

early success stories before securing a venture capitalist audience. Your financial projections also will need to be supported by solid assumptions and be based upon much more than "guesstimates."

2. Bankers. While they likely look at the same success indicators as the above-mentioned group, they obviously are not investing their own money. They are bound by the standards of their lending institution, however. Having a respectable credit rating can't hurt with this bunch.

3. Partners. These individuals are looking for an appropriate match between their own personal interests and what you and your business offer. A potential management team member may possess a core competency skill that you lack yet need (accounting, for example) and share your dream of business ownership. Would-be advisory board members are professionals with narrow yet deep expertise in areas relevant to some aspect of your business. University professors often are called upon to fulfill this role.

4. Employees. As the proprietor of a start-up organization, you may not have the option of hiring people to work for you. Or, given the nature of your business, you may have no choice but to do so. Employees represent a distinct audience group that can make or break the success of your business. Although start-ups are not known for their ability to offer job security, that's precisely what many would-be employees will look for. Alternatively, they may wish to work their way into an ownership position within the business, a concept known as "sweat equity." They'll also look for opportunity for growth, with an assumption that as the business grows and prospers, their role will as well. An undeniable reality of start-up employees is that they are often asked to perform numerous duties and work well outside formal job descriptions. They'll also need to be comfortable with ambiguity, short deadlines, and shifting priorities.

5. Suppliers. It's important to analyze the level of interdependency between your potential suppliers and your business. To what degree is their success contingent on your own, and vice versa? Through that lens this audience group will assess your business's potential, strengths and weaknesses, and likely impact on their own business.

6. Customers. The familiarity of the sales process might make it tempting to view customers as the least daunting audience group. Customer perceptions of your business, however, are arguably your top priority. Perhaps your business idea evolved because as a customer, you could not find what you wanted or needed, or maybe you felt your skills could take an existing product or service and make it better. Feedback from customers at every stage of your business's life cycle is absolutely critical for your success. Be it early-stage focus groups or feedback from repeat customers, careful attention to this audience group should always be an entrepreneur's top priority.

SHOW, DON'T TELL

After spending weeks or months digging down to the gritty details of your business, preparing for your presentation requires that you do exactly the opposite. To tell the compelling story that is unique to your business, you'll need to rise back up to the 35,000-foot level and look at your business from the different perspective of your distinct audience groups. You know more than anyone about your business, which is both a blessing and a curse. It may be tempting to assume knowledge on the part of your audience or take shortcuts in explaining assumptions for why markets exist. After all, you've spent months documenting these "truths"—isn't it only logical that your audience will agree with your assessment? Unfortunately, this is a dangerous assumption that entraps many entrepreneurs. The tendency to jump past rationales for why a business should exist is the first of several temptations you'll need to resist.

Fortunately, presentation software such as Microsoft PowerPoint is a helpful tool in organizing key points for business plan presentations. Its outline-default mode encourages you to structure talking points from the broad to the specific, enabling you to create a story for the audience to follow. When you think of story, don't envision *Gone With the Wind*. Rather, a balance between visuals and text complemented by your selection of talking points is the best approach. PowerPoint is a visual medium, capable of supporting a variety of content treatments. The trick is to select the most supportive approach to represent each section of your business plan.

An important note to mention is the recent trend by investors of asking to review PowerPoint presentations instead of, or in addition to, full business plans. It's worth considering putting together a second set of presentation slides solely for this purpose. What investors are really asking to see is your idea in a nutshell, evidence of a market, and a demonstration of how you plan to make money in that market. As simple as such a request sounds, that information can sometimes get lost in a thirty-page business plan. The default of a bulleted PowerPoint list forces entrepreneurs to make hierarchal decisions about the importance of business variables, effectively deleting nonessential material. The problem is that these presentations tend to be text heavy, meant to be read rather than spoken. The best presentations allow entrepreneurs to combine their verbal explanation with visual representation, so these investor drafts are probably not what you would want to use in front of live audiences. However, if these additional PowerPoint slides serve the purpose of getting a potential investor excited about your idea, then they are worth the time of putting together as a business plan supplement.

As you prepare to discuss your business in front of various audience groups, you'll want to begin the slide development process by visualizing every aspect of your business—from the steps involved in completing a service, to product specifics, to cash flow and audience demographics. Putting this in outline form is often helpful. You'll find that some factors will easily translate into visual components, such as those typically represented on a balance sheet or income statement. Others will be more complex, such as assumptions underlying a business premise that you have incorporated as justification for market share projections.

Don't assume that the way you've previously observed elements presented in presentations is the best or only way to display them here—you have lots of options to work with. Allow your content objectives (what you hope to accomplish by sharing this information with your audience) to determine the appropriate visual display rather than the other way around. After you've made your content choices and decided what visuals you'll need, then you can begin to imagine what they might look like. You have many graphic design elements to work with, including scanned images, maps, logos and icons, pie charts and bar graphs, Web site screen shots, video, and animation. Below are sample content objectives taken from a variety of start-up organizations to jump-start your imagination.

1. CONTENT OBJECTIVE: INTRODUCE YOUR COMPANY

The difficulty of this task is directly related to the type of business you are in. For a company such as WedSteps, an online wedding consulting service, the nature of the business is inherent in the name. Steps of the wedding process are commonly understood, so WedSteps need only explain how it differs from other online wedding service companies. The company needs only one slide to introduce itself and define its services for busy brides to be.

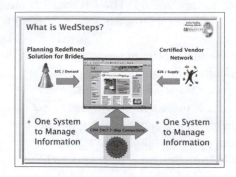

Company introductions become more complicated if your business is in a new or unknown industry or if you've developed a product/service that is not intuitively understandable. That was the case for LiquidWatch, a start-up company that inspects, monitors, and manages restaurant grease trap levels. Unless you're a restaurant owner, you've probably never thought about the potential for mishandling grease associated with food preparation. Poor grease management leads to clogs, backups, and overflows. It also can result in regulatory action or fines for the restaurant, excessive cleanup costs, and bad publicity. In introducing LiquidWatch, the management team needs to explain not only how the grease-pumping process works, but also how its approach is more cost efficient and reliable than current models. This takes several slides but is critical to establishing audience understanding of the business concept. It also provides a nice transition to the next content objective, justifying market demand.

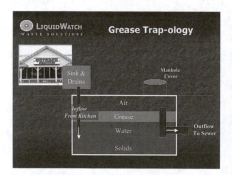  

2. CONTENT OBJECTIVE: JUSTIFICATION OF MARKET DEMAND

You'll need to demonstrate a strong demand for the product/service you plan to provide. One option for achieving this is to document ongoing trends that support your market justifications. In this scenario, you are solving a problem either unmet or underserved by current product and service suppliers. Alternatively, you can show that your approach to meeting this demand is somehow superior to current market options, perhaps by being less expensive or more efficient. This objective is a logical complement to the business introduction and very often follows that section in sequence. Here's how LiquidWatch made the transition from its introduction to its justification of market demand.

You also may want to take a few moments in this section to show where your market is located and how it geographically disperses itself. Highlighted maps are a nice technique for this task, as is a pie chart. Here's how RaceTown used both to show the size of its racetrack market, the locations of the racetracks, and their proximity to one another.

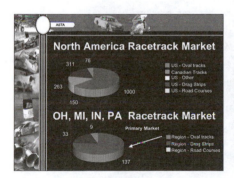

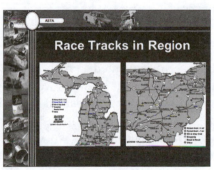

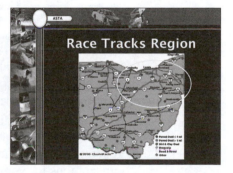

3. CONTENT OBJECTIVE: WHAT PROBLEM DO YOU SOLVE?

If your business justification is that the business solves a problem, it's logical to explain exactly how you plan to do this. You may also need to demonstrate that a legitimate problem really exists. Not that solving nuisances can't make for good business (see the WedSteps model on the next page), but clearly, the former situation creates a more immediate need within your marketplace. For a business such as LiquidWatch, the consequences of not solving the grease trap problem are expensive and potentially threatening to restaurants' abilities to maintain public health standards. Rather than make those claims directly, the LiquidWatch management team opted for external validation from excerpts of newspaper publications about the topic.

The WedSteps business model offers convenience plus the ability to save time and/or money as an approach to solving potential problems for busy brides. The company opts to discuss how it helps busy brides in tandem with a discussion of the online bridal industry because one of its competitive advantages is the lack of similar services in its target market.

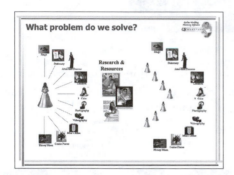 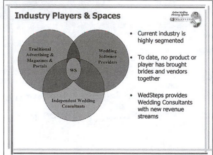

4. CONTENT OBJECTIVE: EXACTLY HOW DOES YOUR PRODUCT OR SERVICE WORK?

Do you have a patent? Have you invented a process? Now is the time to really show your audience how the core competency of your business works. You may use animation to demonstrate steps in a process or a series of slides accompanied by talking points delivered by you or another member of your business team. These slides must be excruciatingly clear—if members of your audience can't understand how your business works, they won't be able to appreciate how you generate revenue. This skepticism is the last thing you want as you begin to explain the financial expectations for your business.

5. CONTENT OBJECTIVE: COMPETITION

A common error for new entrepreneurs is underestimating the breadth and depth of competition. Perhaps there's no other business exactly like your own, but you certainly are competing for the disposable income of your customers. What did they buy before you entered the market? Which companies served their needs? What are the alternatives to your product or service? These are only a few of the questions you should have answered in your feasibility study. During your formal presentation, you'll likely only mention the names of companies you consider to be competitive and offer brief reasons you believe that to be the case. A Q-&-A session may trigger more specific inquiries from audience members, however, so be ready to go into detail about competitors' strengths and weaknesses.

Here's a simple example of how to show who your competition is according to product offerings. ChanaDora's Healthy Delights is a bakery featuring low-fat and diabetic desserts. Its competition includes everything from mainstream national bakeries with high supermarket visibility to local bakeries that offer specialty products.

6. CONTENT OBJECTIVE: FINANCIAL FORECASTS

Probably the most difficult section of the presentation will be that devoted to financial information: start-up costs, sales and sales projections, and pro forma information (anticipated expenses, revenue, and income). A basic guideline is to move from the general to the specific as you explain your calculations and estimates. It's far easier for most audience groups to follow the reasoning (also called assumptions) that justifies your projections if you work from the macro to the micro level. This approach also will help you avoid putting too much information on a single slide—a tendency that also can overwhelm an audience. A progression of slides is your best choice, with each slide offering a deeper level of detail than the previous one.

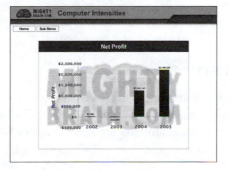

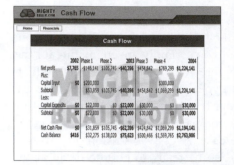
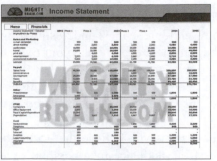
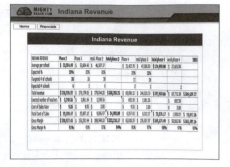

Also, just because this is the financial section of your presentation doesn't mean that it has to look like a balance sheet or income statement that you'd read in an annual report. ChanaDora's Healthy Delights found a unique yet effective technique using a series of Power-Point builds to display its start-up costs and expected sales.

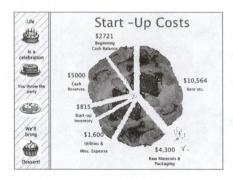
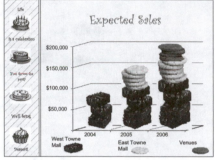

Finally, if the purpose of your presentation is to request funding, it's a good idea to devote a slide to how much you are seeking and how the funds will be used. A simple text slide can get this job done clearly and effectively.

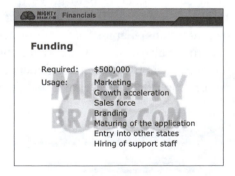

7. CONTENT OBJECTIVE: MILESTONES

You will need to demonstrate how you will implement your business plan, including a timeline for when you expect to reach certain goals. These milestones can be displayed in a number of ways. The only two essential elements are dates and goals. A good approach involves showing where and how goals overlap and what required steps are assumed along the way. Typically, milestones extend from the present to three to five years in the future. As you can see below, RaceTown's timeline demonstrates how major year-end goals are supported by short-term, yet critical accomplishments.

Your milestones also may be extended to show how customers may evolve as they use your product and/or service. In the case of WedSteps, the company faced an obvious challenge to sustaining a base of repeat customers. To answer the question "So what happens after the wedding?" the company extended its milestones to include services for newlyweds and then new parents. The two-slide sequence explains how the company plans to continue to grow and expand and helps make the milestones appear more attainable.

8. CONTENT OBJECTIVE: THE Q-&-A SESSION

An effective way to prepare for any persuasive speaking opportunity (and if you're looking for investment dollars, this certainly qualifies) is to anticipate the types of questions your audience is likely to ask. If you are a nervous presenter, you may find it comforting to develop slides with material that supports logical questions for your audience to ask. This exercise also helps you check your presentation (and business plan) for completeness. Supplemental slides also give you the option of customizing your presentation on a moment's notice by simply changing the slide order using PowerPoint's slide sorter feature. The challenge is to keep track of all your slides so that you can find the appropriate data for responding to specific questions. One approach used by MightyBrain, an online educational support company for teachers, students, and parents, makes extensive use of hyperlinks within related slide material. By organizing material by major categories and then clustering related slides within each category, Mighty-Brain presenters can move quickly and seamlessly though large volumes of support material.

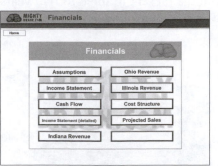

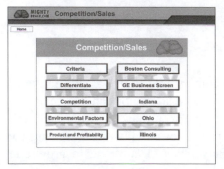

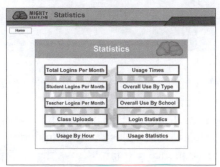

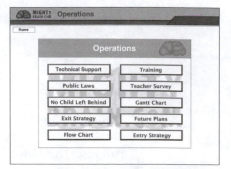

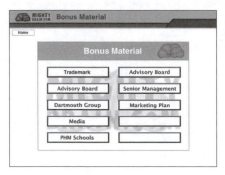

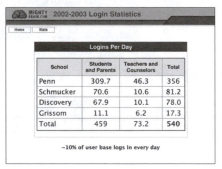

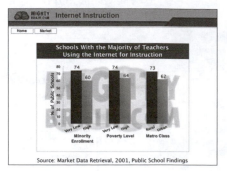

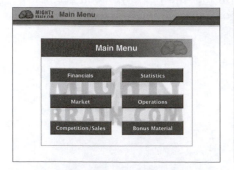

ORGANIZING YOUR PRESENTATION

Your slide sequence is directly related to the specific group in your audience and how much time you have to spend with them. Chapter 5 will further define strategies for talking with various audience groups and incorporating their feedback into your business. For now, let's focus on a typical sequence of slides for a presentation to an audience of would-be investors. This is by no means a mandatory order—just a dozen slides that work well in many speaking situations.

1. Cover slide
2. Problem/solution description
3. Executive summary or mission statement
4. Description of product/service
5. Description of market
6. Overview of competition

7. Go-to-market strategy
8. Timeline for milestones
9. Financial forecast
10. Management team credentials
11. Exit strategy
12. Conclusion and call for questions

FINISHING TOUCHES

Much as you'd edit a text document prior to submission, you also need to carefully review your PowerPoint slides for a number of critical factors.

1. Readability. Is the type and font legible? Can your audience clearly see the numbers contained in tables and charts? Can those sitting in the back row read the text without squinting? (If you don't have an answer for this, try to make it readable from about 20 feet.) Type that is too large also can be distracting, as can too much of any size of type on a single slide.
2. Visual impact. The goal is not to underwhelm your audience. Does your presentation convey the energy and excitement that investors look for in entrepreneurs? If your presentation needs jazzing up, trying adding text or image builds, color, or perhaps a bit of animation or video to the story. Avoid the long lists of dates, long lists of bullets, and long lists in general.
3. Overkill. Does your presentation go too far? For example, just because you can include audio in your presentations doesn't mean you want to. Sure, if you're in the music business, audio makes sense—but sound clips that herald the arrival of every slide can become annoying quickly.
4. Completeness. You'd use a focus group to generate feedback on your product or service, so why not also do so with your presentation? You want to be sure that you're not leaving out material that the audience really wants to see and that the material you've included is what the audience really cares about. Use friends, family, roommates—anyone willing to sit still for about twenty minutes and remain objective can work here.
5. Clutter. The most likely candidates for information overload are the financial section and graphics that try to squeeze too much information onto a single slide. Overall comprehension will be better if you take several slides and build on key points rather than jamming lots of data, text, and visuals onto a single slide. That approach makes the audience members work too hard because they are forced to repeatedly scan their eyes back and forth over the material to determine meaning. Sometimes less really is more. To paraphrase an old expression, "When in doubt, leave it out" (but put it in the Q-&-A slide section just in case).

REVIEW

You should now have some ideas for how to design professional slides that have visual impact. Always begin with your audience in mind, and be cognizant of any time restrictions on your speaking window. Let your content drive the selection of visual media rather than the other way around. Be sure to try out your presentation. Get feedback on whether it really shows the story of your business and answers potential questions of your audience.

ASSIGNMENTS

1. Create a storyboard for your presentation. This is a visual outline of how you envision your presentation to look. Try out different visual packages (pie charts, maps, bar charts, etc.) to see which medium conveys your data in the most interesting and compelling manner.

2. Create a "master slide" to use as a backdrop for all your related presentation material. This slide should incorporate any logos or product images you wish others to associate with your business. Experiment with colors and fonts until you find a combination that best represents how you wish others to perceive your business.

3. Even if you haven't finished your business plan, go ahead and begin to draft your presentation slides. You needn't work on these slides in any given sequence because their order is easily changed. Simply be sure that every major section of your business plan section has at least one corresponding slide in your presentation (for some sections, you'll likely have two to three slides or even more).

4. Try practicing your presentation with different time variations. Develop separate ten-, twenty-, and thirty-minute versions. Practice in front of an audience to gather feedback and gain experience in answering questions.

ENDNOTES

1. J. S. O'Rourke, *Management Communication: A Case-Analysis Approach,* 2nd ed. (Upper Saddle River, NJ: Prentice Hall, 2004), 99–100.

5 TALK AND LISTEN TO THOSE WHO CAN HELP

"Statistics are no substitute for judgment."

—Henry Clay

Be it a ride on a venture capital road show or a quick trip up an elevator, the next phase of your new business development will certainly keep you moving. This is one of the most exhilarating aspects of starting a business: sharing your dream with others. Not only will your plan fall under tremendous scrutiny during this phase, but so will your ability to lead and manage your business. A good idea is only that, unless the person designated to execute it has the skills, savvy, patience, and persistence to finish what was started in developing the feasibility study and writing the business plan. That person is you, but you'll need to convince other key audience groups of that fact if you hope to obtain their support as you proceed from here.

Chapter 5 will help you accomplish these goals. In this chapter, we will review common venues for business plan presentations, from elevator pitches, to competitions, to potential investor meetings. We'll also further discuss the presentation process, with a special emphasis on how to appeal to the needs of the audience groups you are most likely to encounter.

ELEVATOR PITCHES: NOT JUST FOR ELEVATORS ANYMORE

Although the idea of running into someone in an elevator sounds like the ultimate impromptu speaking opportunity, it is really necessary to give this chance meeting some serious thought in advance. Networking options exist everywhere, so having a concise but effective way to explain your new business is definitely in your best interest. You never know who you might meet while standing in a line at a coffee shop, whether they'd be interested in your plans, or whether they know others to whom they could refer you. There's even an annual competition for elevator pitches hosted by the Babcock Graduate School of Management at Wake Forest University. Be it completely spontaneous or a bit more formal, you certainly wouldn't want a great networking opportunity to slip through your fingers only because you couldn't figure out what to say. Memorizing a thirty-second shorthand version of your business plan just makes good sense. Have longer variations of the pitch ready to go as well, from sixty seconds to as long as four minutes (just in case you find yourself riding the elevator in Chicago's Sears Tower).

So what are the ingredients of an effective elevator pitch? You won't close any deals during this conversation—all you can hope to accomplish is to generate an initial interest and try to obtain an opportunity for a longer follow-up discussion. Keep everything simple and conversational—this is no time to review the intricacies of your competitive analysis or test out your thesaurus. Answer the basic questions: What is the heart and core of your business, and why will it be successful? Remind yourself that enthusiasm and energy often are contagious and go a long way in obtaining subsequent appointments. Following are several additional elements you'll want to think about as you draft your elevator pitch.

1. What problem does your business solve? Alternatively, what opportunities does it create? Does it save time, money, or both?
2. Why should anyone care? How has your targeted market(s) gotten along until now? How does your product/service simplify or enhance your market's lives in some positive manner?
3. What is special or unique in your approach to this business? Do you have skills or experience that you can draw on to make improvements in the status quo? In a succinct fashion, you'll need to explain why you are credible and why the person you're speaking with should believe your pitch.
4. Is your pitch motivating? Why would the person you are speaking with want to set aside additional time with you to learn more?
5. Can you make money doing this? Show early successes in terms of sales, product demand, and customer feedback about potential improvements to product and services.
6. Can you prove everything you just said? How have you established your credibility with your customers in terms of product and service guarantees? Who can offer references on your behalf? Are there sources of third-party credibility (analysts or the media) that can verify your market size, business impact, and sales potential?

In keeping with all these factors, you need to caution yourself against what start-up business mentor Dave Brenner calls "pitch decay." As comanaging partner of the Grand Rapids, Michigan-based entrepreneurial consulting firm IdeaWorks, Brenner has counseled thousands of entrepreneurs over the past thirty years. The experience and expertise of IdeaWorks lies in new business venture formation and development, strategic analysis and planning, sales and marketing, new products and services development, and new market intelligence. Brenner and his partner, Tom Edwards, counsel new businesses from the start-up through implementation stages of development. Based upon his experience, Brenner knows that trying to jam too much information into too small a time frame will only backfire and hurt your cause for support.

Pitch decay means that most audiences only remember half of what they hear within a given hour, which drops to a recollection rate of 20 percent by the end of the day. By the end of the week, most audiences will have forgotten 90 percent of what you said. So you must make it your business to figure out your talking points beforehand, and keep hitting them hard throughout the discussion. Talking points are the few essentials that you want people to remember about your business, no matter what.[1]

Finally, you also are responsible for establishing closure for the elevator conversation. This means that you'll inquire about setting up an appointment to speak further—in person or by telephone—at a later date. Be sure to print professional business cards and carry them everywhere. They provide a convenient means to share contact information. Offer your card, extend a handshake, and thank the person for the time they have spent with you, no matter how brief. If you've been invited to initiate follow-up opportunities, do so at your earliest convenience.

Here's a sample elevator pitch to get you started:

Good morning, Mr./Ms./Dr. Satchel. I recognize you from your cable television show "KidSmart" on Sunday afternoons on WMBT. My name is Melissa Simmons, and I'm president of ABC Kids. We develop and publish education tools for children with autism and other types of learning disabilities. We offer workbooks and flashcards for children, newsletters for their parents and teachers, and even video programs intended to help doctors and other medical professionals become knowledgeable in how to treat these children. Our best-selling title, Teach your Child to Read and Count in 90 Days, was named Book of the Year by the state Parent-Teacher Association."

VENTURE OR BUSINESS PLAN COMPETITIONS

If you are a student at the secondary, undergraduate, or graduate levels, or even an alumnus of business degree-granting institutions, you likely have access to business or venture plan competitions. These are formal competitions that give you a chance to compete for cash awards, access to venture capitalists, high product and service visibility, and public relations, or all the above. Palo Alto Software President Tim Berry explains the distinctions between a venture and business plan competition, although many programs use the two terms interchangeably:

Venture competitions are more common and more fashionable than business plan competitions. These competitions evaluate the venture's chances for success based on factors such as market, competitive advantage, financing, and management team.

They should always include presentations for judges, and question-and-answer (Q-&-A) sessions. While plans are used for screening entrants, the presentations are usually even more important. Judges use presentations and Q-&-A responses to evaluate the management team, a critical factor. It takes an excellent plan to get into the final rounds, and an excellent presentation to win.

A business plan competition, on the other hand, is based on the document itself. Judges use the plan as the summary of the entire venture—the same factors perhaps as the venture contest, but the judgment is based on the document alone—there is no presentation.[2]

You'll find numerous opportunities to become involved in these events, although many have criteria that you must meet beforehand. Arguably, the most prestigious competition is the by-invitation-only Moot Corp., sponsored each May by the McCombs School of Business at the University of Texas at Austin. Called "The Super Bowl of World Business Plan Competitions" by *Business Week,* this 20-year-old annual event is open only to first-prize recipients of other approved competitions affiliated with MBA programs around the world. Awards include $100,000 in cash prizes to top finishers, and participants have the opportunity to meet (and deal) with prominent venture capitalists, many of whom serve as judges.

While the majority of competitions are associated with academic programs, the Small Business Administration[3] offers similar experiences throughout the country, as do some state and regional government offices. Presented in Table 5–1 are lists of prominent business competitions in the United States, The key features offered by major competitions appear in Table 5–2. A list of additional competitions is found in Appendix B.

Table 5.1 Major U.S. MBA Business Plan Competitions	
Competition Host	**Competition Name and Date**
University of Georgia	**Georgia Bowl® Competition** First or second week of February
Indiana University	**Spirit of Enterprise Competition** Third week of February
University of California Santa Barbara	S.E.E.D. Business Plan Competition Early spring
University of Nebraska	**Info-USA Business Plan Competition** Fourth week of February
Carnegie Mellon University	**International Business Plan Competition** March
Boise State University	**Northwest Business Plan Competition** March
San Diego State University	**International Venture Challenge™** March
Wake Forest University	The Elevator Competition Fourth week of March
Rice University	**Southwest Business Plan Competition** March
University of San Francisco	**International Business Plan Competition** April
University of Oregon	**New Venture Championship** Second or third week of April
Purdue University	Life Sciences Competition Third week of April
Carrot Capital	*Carrot Capital Business Plan Challenge* April
MBA Jungle	*MBA Jungle Business Plan Competition* April
University of Texas	International Challenge of Moot Corp® First or second week of May

Key: Competitions listed in regular type are hosted by academic institutions.
        Competitions listed in italic type are hosted by nonacademic organizations.
        Competitions listed in bold type send their winners to Moot Corp®.

Source: "AACSB International." Retrieved July 10, 2004 from http://www.aacsb.edu/conferences/.

Table 5.2   Key Features of U.S. MBA Business Plan Competitions

Competition	Competition Focus and Uniqueness
Georgia Bowl® Competition (first or second week of February)	Its unique scoring system focuses on actual startup feasibility. Top two semifinalists in each bracket go to finals.
Indiana Spirit of Enterprise Competition (third week of February)	A one-day competition that emphasizes reality in the plan's details. If your numbers are wrong, you're gone.
S.E.E.D. Business Plan Competition (third week of February)	A new competition that deemphasizes the team's written plan. Focuses on feasibility and venture upside potential.
Nebraska Info-USA Competition (fourth week of February)	Third oldest national competition. Focuses on start-up feasibility. Holds an undergraduate competition at the same time.
Carnegie International Competition (first week of March)	A new competition. Focus is not yet clear.
Boise State Northwest Competition (third week of March)	Second newest competition. Open to eight northwestern schools plus "at large" entries. Holds undergraduate competition at the same time.
SDSU International Venture Challenge™ (third week of March)	Second oldest national competition. Has wild-card opportunity for all second-place teams to advance to finals. Has five open slots.

continued

Competition	Competition Focus and Uniqueness
Wake Forest Elevator Competition (fourth week of March)	Make two pitches in two two-minute elevator rides to advance to finals and do a full pitch to four North Carolina venture capitalists. Nonstudents okay in finals.
Rice Southwest Competition (fourth week of March)	Strong venture capital emphasis. Fifteen-plus judges in all first-round brackets. Best #2 gets wild card to finals. Forty-five + final-round judges, mostly venture capitalists.
USF International Competition (first week of April)	Plans deemphasized. Elevator pitch to venture capitalists to determine semifinal brackets. Finalists pitch to California venture capitalist panel.
Oregon New Venture Championship (second or third week of April)	Environmentally friendly plans favored. Has prize for best fast pitch presentation. All slots except five are open to any school.
Purdue Life Sciences Competition (third week of April)	All entrants must qualify on written plans. Emphasis is on biotechnology, medical devices, and health services.
Carrot Capital Business Plan Challenge (fourth weekend of April)	Must submit business plans. The top twelve teams invited to New York City for presentations. Most top teams are offered term sheets.
MBA Jungle Business Plan Competition (fourth week of April)	Must submit executive summaries to MBA Jungle. Top teams are invited to California for the competition.
International Challenge of Moot Corp® (first or second week of May)	The biggest and oldest of them all. $100,000 convertible preferred loan to winner to help get venture started.

Key: Competitions listed in regular type are hosted by academic institutions.
           Competitions listed in italic type are hosted by nonacademic organizations.
           Competitions listed in bold type send their winners to Moot Corp®.

Source: "ACSB International." Retrieved from http://www.aacsb.edu/conferences/.

MEETINGS WITH POTENTIAL INVESTORS

As mentioned in Chapter 4, not all investors are created equal. Venture capitalists often consolidate resources in funds or firms and often are professionally managed and industry specific. Angel investors are high-net-worth individuals who may be considering an investment of their private funds or work as a member of a smaller consortium or a fund collective. As an audience group, they share characteristics of being direct, extremely busy, and impatient with fluff, spin, or conjecture. A meeting with this audience is certainly a big step in the right direction, but it's a long way from guaranteed funding. In fact, guarantees are few and far between—you may not even have five minutes to present your formal presentation before this group before being interrupted with questions. Increasingly, this audience group also is forgoing a total review of your business plan in favor of a copy of your PowerPoint slides and an attached executive summary. Without a doubt, your survival and success before this group will depend on being specific yet succinct.

No one knows that better than Tim Connors, a partner with U.S. Venture Partners (USVP), a Menlo Park, California–based venture capital firm focusing on investments in industries that include communications, software, semiconductors, and the Internet. Since its inception in 1981, USVP has raised more than $2.9 billion in nine funds, including a $600 million fund that closed in January 2005.

Connors specializes in building enterprise software and semiconductor companies with a primary focus on seed/early-stage companies.[4] Following is his perspective of what he looks for in a pitch.

A Great Venture Capital Pitch

Connors says, "PowerPoint presentations create an outline for a business. I'd recommend preparing this first—even before you write the executive summary and certainly before you write your business plan. Then you can get feedback on your PowerPoint pitch, hone the business idea, and then commit to writing a business plan. The PowerPoint pitch will often be the first document that you produce to gain attention from a broad set of potential investors. Focus on internal content rather than fancy pictures. Every picture should have a reason for existing. If you can say it on one line, do it. No more than six major bullets per page, with none extending more than a single line." Connors sees so many plans that he's developed a guide for entrepreneurs on the thought process of venture capitalists. He's convinced that the likelihood of a successful meeting with venture capitalists would increase if more applicants understand their perspective. He shares his thoughts in the table below, offering a glimpse into how venture capitalists think about each major section of the business plan.

Table 5.3	What Venture Capitalists Think About Your Plan
Slide	Description
Mission statement	The one-liner for the company
Market	Your total available market; what your revenue would be if you got 100 percent of your target customers paying what you expect
Customer's problem you are solving	Who is the customer? Do they matter? What problem does the customer have today? Why is that a big problem? Why is it their biggest problem?
How you solve customer's problem	What is your solution? Why is it unique? Why has nobody done this before? What does their income statement look like before and after your solution? Do you "move the needle?" Is it enabling them to do something they couldn't do before? Does it deliver five times to ten times better/faster/cheaper?
Technology status	If big IP piece, several slides on the state of your tech development
Customer status	Who has agreed to pay for the product? Who are betas? Etc.

What I'm Thinking	Best Answer
Okay. Looked at ten companies today. What am I going to be looking at for the next hour. Why should I be enthused?	I can see an analogy to a past winner. "Yahoo! for X industry," or "Cisco for Y industry," etc.
Is this market big enough to yield a highly valued company? Is it growing fast? Are there changes that are making room for start-ups and making the entrenched companies nervous?	Need opportunity for > $1 billion in revenues in a high-margin business; high growth; disruptions creating opportunities for new players
Will customers care about this product and company? Are the customers significant? Do they have all the power and a reputation for being friendly to start-ups? Are the customers "good" customers? Companies that sell to high-gross-margin customers tend to have high gross margins. Those that sell to low-gross-margin customers have low gross margins.	Most important problem for customers who are high-gross-margin, high-growth companies in high-growth sectors who move very quickly and frequently buy products from start-ups
Is it unique? What has changed that allows room for a start-up here? Is there an impact big enough to survive the corporate procurement cycle?	You have come up with a solution that you found because of exclusive domain expertise that is really hard for others to match. You deliver at least 100 basis points of incremental net income for companies that matter. Your solution is sufficiently differentiated to allow a risk-averse customer to take a risk on buying your product.
Is there a lot of research left, lots of development left, or is the product done?	All the risk of research is done; no major unsolved technical problems remain.
Are there customers who matter with high willingness to pay?	Referenceable customers who are falling over to get the product; if the product is in beta, at least one customer is seeing big impact with it.

continued

Slide	Description
Go-to-market strategy	How will you get in front of the customer—direct, indirect, etc.? What is the method and cost of selling?
Per-customer economics	What they will pay, what it costs to service them, what it costs to acquire them
Team	Top six to seven people with one sub-bullet on relevant past; why this is a world-class team with relevant skills to pull this off; why they can recruit from their networks. What have they done before that is special? Have they done it before, or are they learning as they go?
Financials	Past two and next two quarters, next year, two years out, three years out across the horizontal axis: number of customers, big revenue lines, COGS, gross margin, big expense lines, net income, cash flow, cumulative cash flow
Competition overview	Two-by-two matrix of the competition with the two variables that matter on the X and Y
Competition specifics	The top two or three competitors, one- or two-liner on their story (funding, etc), one- or two-liner on why you beat them

What I'm Thinking	Best Answer
Is there a channel that can allow this company to get their product to customers profitably? Anyone in the way to this start-up reaching their customers?	Product falls off the shelf fast; very easy, short sales cycle sell.
What information does this round of capital buy?	Big milestones will be hit quickly that allow big step-up in valuation next round.
Do I want to talk to these people every other day for the next five years and every month for the next ten years?	Done it before; recruiting is easy; key team in place. Success follows all these guys, yet they are hungry for a defining moment in their careers in building a world-class company. As Warren Buffett says, "Would I be comfortable having my daughter or son marry this person?"
How are the gross margins (how competitive)? How quickly does the company ramp? How many dollars to profitability? Do these guys understand how a company ramps? Are they believable numbers?	Healthy ramp—not too many dollars and not too long to profitability; great gross margins; realistic numbers.
How is the company positioned in the landscape with all the other companys I've seen? How are companies in this category valued? Do I know about competitors that these guys don't have listed, or are these guys clued in on their competition?	No big uglies with the start-up directly in their sights; not a bunch of money already invested by other venture capitalists in companies attacking the same space.
Do I believe these guys can win? Who are the couple to focus due diligence efforts on? Is it an area with big market caps?	No one else has raised significant money yet. An underserved segment. Big market cap guys around the area (but weak in this segment) that validate the space and help with big market caps on IPO or acquisition.

continued

Slide	Description
Financing history/deal	How much went in so far? When? At what price? Who are current investors? How much do they own? Who is on the board? How much are you raising now, and at what price? What is the cap table? How big is the unallocated pool?
Why this firm?	Why you want us as investors.

Table 5.4   The Sixteen Attributes of the Perfect Enterprise Software Investment

1. Great team . . . history of great execution combined with great strategic navigation
   Execution risk is huge in software
2. Version 1.0 of the software is done . . . and scalable
   Can be traded away for a great team . . . but at a lower valuation/staged investment
3. Hard ROI . . . with validation
   "Easy to measure and to explain to potential customers, employees, partners, investors"
   At least one great customer who believes and is buying
4. Global2000 customers
   "Avoid small business, avoid mid-market if they can't also serve the big guys."
5. "Direct sales channel price points of six figures initially, approaching seven figures in out years"
6. Eager indirect channel partners with mid-five-figure deals growing to six-figure price points
7. No big uglies with their sights directly pointed at the startup
8. Scales to 75 percent-plus gross margins
   Requires good mix of license versus services
   No ASPs who simply resell others' software

continued

What I'm Thinking	Best Answer
Is cap table in good shape? Are there helpful people around the company? Do I know any of the investors whose opinion I trust?	Strong preference if this is the first round of capitalization in the company. If not first round, the team gave away less than 15 percent to the first-round guys. First-round guys are helpful, reasonable characters who've helped the company get its DNA right. First-round guys are guys we know and respect and want to work with who can give us a quick read on the pros/cons of the opportunity.
What are their motivations?	Focused on getting the right investor rather than highest first-round valuation. Understand our portfolio and where the particular fits are and what introductions we can make. Understand what we are good at and are realistic about how we can help.

9. Solves one of the top three pain points for the target VP/CEO
    "If not, will never get the necessary attention, and sales cycles will be long."
10. "Sector not well understood, overhyped, overfunded by venture capitalists"
    "When five other venture capitalists or the 'red herring' claim the area is 'hot,' run away!"
11. Market size: clear path to $1 billion in revenue
    "May not get there, but the opportunity is big enough to go after with real $$."
12. Some market disruption that is occuring to create room for a start-up
    "Timing, timing, timing."
    "A new standard, changes in the customers, etc."
13. Solves problems for more than one vertical
    "The initial vertical is a get-to-market strategy, not the entire business."
14. Touches lots of people in the target customer
    Lots of seats = very sticky
15. Software is delivered behind the firewall . . .
    Or have a great reason for why it is hosted.
16. The target customers are good customers
    People who sell to low-gross-margin customers tend to have low gross margins.

QUESTIONS AND ANSWERS ON Q-&-A

As Tim Berry mentioned, venture plan competitions often incorporate question-and-answer components into the presentation requirement. It is essential that you prepare for this speaking opportunity as much as for the formal presentation, but in a different manner and with different goals. Berry suggests that your tone and choice of words can be as important as the information you choose to share. He cautions: "Beware of extremes because they don't work. These include:

- "The extreme submissive strategy, thanking people for their objections and promising to take them into consideration
- "The extreme defensive strategy, defending every point to the death despite all logic and reason
- "The extreme aggressive strategy, arguing with the judges"[5]

"Strive for a middle ground, between the extremes, that respects the judges and honors the truth," Berry continues. "When in doubt, look for the truth in the points of view, and follow the truth to the right answer. Sometimes judges' objections will be the most valuable lesson you'll learn in the contest.

GUIDELINES FOR SUCCESSFUL PRESENTATIONS

Regardless of speaking venue or purpose, you should keep in mind a number of common "do's and don'ts" as you proceed with your presentations. It's not enough to simply have a great idea committed to paper with the statistics to back it up—it's time to sell that idea and convince your audience that you and your team are the best choice to make this business a reality. Yes, you've done all the hard work, but no, you can't hide behind it. Here are a dozen "dos and don'ts" strategies to help increase your likelihood of presentation success.

DO'S

1. Make it personal. Try to find out as much as you can about each individual you will be speaking to beforehand. At a minimum, know names and titles. If possible, introduce yourself personally to each audience member before you begin to speak. Gathering helpful anecdotes such as where they live or attended school also can give you options for personalizing presentation content to the group.
2. Be organized. Tell your audience in advance how you plan to proceed through your presentation by giving them a road map in the form of an agenda or overview slide. This need not take more than ninety seconds, but it helps them organize the sequence of events about to unfold. You may want to consider using a "frames" approach to your PowerPoint presentation, designating a margin of each slide as a miniature outline for key discussion points.
3. Be considerate of their time. Tell them how long you will speak, and then keep your word. In general, shorter is generally better, and by short we're talking ten to twenty minutes. If more time is available, allow your audience to drive the discussion by offering

lots of time for questions and answers. You should know that many investors will be unlikely to allow you to finish your formal presentation before beginning to ask questions. You'll need to adjust your format quickly to adapt to their expectations. Having smaller, interchangeable PowerPoint options enables you to change gears quickly without appearing disorganized or confused. Certainly, this approach allows your audience to see firsthand how you handle stress.

4. Open and close strongly. First impressions are vitally important in entrepreneurial speaking opportunities. Simplify your business idea so that your audience can get excited about it quickly, and then rally your audience around the key factors of market impact, demand, and profitability. It is your job to concisely explain elements to which you may have devoted dozens of pages in your business plan. It is also your job to connect the dots within your business plan—don't make your audience guess how one aspect relates to another. Most importantly, speak in clear, plain English—no technical gobbledygook, acronyms, or insider jargon. Use the strongest speakers on your management team to present your material in the main presentation—content experts (marketing, sales, accounting, etc.) always can be called upon later to answer more technical questions. Finally, be sure to close each segment of your presentation with a strong summary of key points. Don't force your audience to remember what you assume to be most relevant, and don't assume that the audience's definition of relevance is automatically the same as your own.

5. Capture your audience with content. As mentioned in Chapter 4, you want to show off your product or service whenever possible in a presentation. Got a prototype? Bring it. Have a Web site? Link to it. Can a video clip capture the spirit of your new venture? Show it. Demonstrate the impact of your product/service on your chosen market with written testimonials from actual customers (or focus group members). Offer credible evidence to support why your product/service is needed within the market(s) you plan to enter. In short, do whatever it takes to show that you have long surpassed the "idea" stage and have evolved into a real, visible business with bona fide products/services actually engaged in the marketplace. Be sure to convincingly answer the critical questions that any investor would ask: "Who needs this and why?" and "Why you? Why now?"

6. Exude enthusiasm and confidence. No one in the room should be more excited than you are to discuss this material. Use lots of eye contact, and connect with everyone in the room at least once. Be sure your speaking voice is strong and clear. Watch that your pace of speech isn't too rapid (nerves can accelerate speaking rates) or monotone—you want your audience to neither struggle to keep up with you nor lose interest.

7. Be Q-&-A savvy. Yes, this point is listed multiple times because it so often makes or breaks meetings with investors. Each audience member has an agenda, which often reveals itself through the choice of questions asked. These questions are actually clues as to the concerns about your business that exist for your audience. Your answers either help allay these fears or compound audience concerns, so be sure it's the former. Ample preparation for presentations can help you anticipate many likely questions and subsequent answers, which can only work to have you appear more organized and professional. However, be sure to really listen to all questions and answer what is actually asked of you, rather than solely relying on what you have prepared for support materials.

DON'TS

1. Don't assume anything. Be sure all your assertions are backed up with generous amounts of research and documentation. For example, if the success of your business is contingent upon a market growth of 5 percent, be sure your can specify exactly when, why, and how that growth will occur, and be ready to provide the baseline from which you derived that figure. If you can't, your audience will likely see right through you, doubt your credibility, and begin to ask some extremely probing questions to challenge your understanding of the premises for your other business decisions.

   Conversely, don't assume that your audience automatically knows as much or more than you in any given area. If you are presenting with a team, assign a nonspeaking member to scan faces in the audience for signs of confusion, disagreement, or overkill. That person can then subtly relay to you that your presentation needs to shift course to better meet the needs of your audience.

2. Don't forget the rightful place of slide material in presentations. You are not speaking to support material presented on your slides—just the opposite. If the audience members didn't want to hear from you, they could have simply requested an e-mailed set of slides (this sometimes happens, by the way). Sure, the slides look great, and you spent a lot of time on their design, but they don't hold the real power here—you do. So don't allocate more power to your slides than they warrant. Don't distribute copies of your slides beforehand—doing so gives your audience an excuse to look at paper copies versus the real thing. Also, feel free to skip a slide or make jumps in sequence if you suspect that the material, as prepared, is not the best fit for a particular audience.

3. Don't usurp your own intelligence. You know more about your business than anyone else in the room, so why make it appear otherwise by clinging to note cards while you speak? Have faith in your ability to remember what you need to, when you need to. If you absolutely cannot give up the note cards, at least save them for the far more detailed information that is likely to be conveyed in a Q-&-A session.

4. Don't use your slides as notes to remember what to say next. Putting down note cards sometimes triggers a tendency to speak with your back to members of your audience, and you "read" your slides. Please don't talk to the projection screen; it can't help you acquire funding. Sure, a quick glance here and there is fine, but keep in mind that this presentation is really a conversation with people who are deciding whether a partnership with you makes sense. To make that decision, they need to get to know you better, and it's hard to do that if you are not speaking directly to them.

5. Don't cram too much of anything onto a single slide. A shorter presentation time doesn't mean taking the same material and bundling it on fewer slides. Sometimes it's easier for audiences to understand complex concepts if they are broken across more slides with ample white space, rather than reduced to a single slide. What's most important is com-prehension—sometimes that's better served by spending ten seconds per three simple slides versus thirty seconds on a more complex one.

6. Don't simply read your slides—interpret them. There are a number of reasons for this. First of all, reading anything verbatim only works to put your audience to sleep. They're all capable readers—why do they need you to do that for them? Rather, use text bullet points as springboards to catapult you into new and interesting content areas for discussion.

You'll also build a lot of credibility with your audience if you can thoroughly walk them through the particulars of the way things work, and why, in your business. After all, no one should know that better than you, and you are demonstrating such. Also, leaving your audience members to interpret data on their own can be dangerous. They may draw conclusions that are inconsistent with your own. Finally, if your audience needs to work too hard to decipher your financial data or graphics, then it's more likely to tune out for the remainder of your presentation and therefore less likely to really pay attention to what you are saying.

Interview with David Brenner, CEO, IdeaWorks, L.L.C., Grand Rapids, Michigan

"If you just remember one thing about presenting your business plan, it should be the 'Five Breath Test.' The idea is that you should be able to convey all of this information succinctly, in just five breaths. Here's what you need to know and be able to communicate to any audience group and any time:

1. What is your idea?
2. "Who needs it, and why?
3. "Why choose you, or this company?
4. "Why now?
5. "How will this company and its investors make money?

"Stick to the basics when crafting your pitch. Here are few guidelines we've assembled from venture capitalists to help you get started.

1. Be brief and to the point.
2. Pitch One Single Idea with passion.
3. Bait the hook vs. Telling the Story.
4. Kill MBA or Geek Speak—speak Plain English.
5. Tap their interest level. . . . "tell me more."
6. Zero in on most obvious market niche.
7. Quantify 'pain' in terms of true market opportunity—*bring it to life*.
8. Tell how market deals with 'pain' now.
9. Clarify what the market really wants.
10. Connect the listener to the problem."[6]

CONCLUSION

Presentations really are a lot of fun. The common denominator is content, but the variance in audience groups will require that each presentation be unique. Keep in mind that no one knows your business as well as you, and no one could possibly be more passionate about it. Don't be afraid to let go of your notes and go with the flow and energy in the room. Also, don't become defensive during Q-&-A sessions because the insights garnered during these discussions offer fresh and valuable perspectives from highly intelligent people. Keep an open mind, but don't lose sight of your dreams.

REVIEW

At least three distinct presentation opportunities are associated with new business development: the elevator pitch, the venture/business plan competition, and meetings with potential investors. Each presentation opportunity comes with a unique set of requirements for preparation and implementation, although common "do's and don'ts" exist for creating an effective presentation style.

ASSIGNMENTS

1. Develop three versions of an elevator pitch—one timed for thirty seconds, another for one minute, and a third for three minutes. Practice each pitch until the words flow comfortably and you are confident that you could deliver them any place at any time.

2. Identify competitions with criteria that you already have met or would likely be able to meet over the next twelve months. The lists within this chapter and at the end of this book will help you get started. Once you've determined deadlines for competition(s) for which you are eligible, build a work schedule "to-do" list backward from the date for initial submissions. Some competitions require participants to submit entire business plans, and others ask for only executive summaries at the preliminary stages. Developing a spreadsheet to show which documents are required by each competition on which dates is an approach that often proves helpful.

3. Conduct an Internet search to develop a list of venture capitalists with areas of specialization related to your new business. Use this research to learn all that you can about key partners, past funding success stories, and requirements to initiate a potential investment meeting opportunity.

ENDNOTES

1. Dave Brenner, telephone interview, July 21, 2004.
2. Tim Berry, "Business Plans and Venture Competitions." White paper published in tandem with release of Business Plan Pro, Palo Alto Software, 2002. Used with permission.
3. "Office of Entrepreneurial Development." Retrieved July 23, 2004 from http://www.sba.gov/sbdc/.
4. "USVP—Our Team—Partners." Retrieved June 29, 2004 from http://www.usvp.com/team/connors.html.
5. Berry, *supra* n.2.
6. Dave Brenner, personal interview, August 1, 2004.

SAMPLE BUSINESS PLAN: MONTROSE URGENT CARE FACILITY

TABLE OF CONTENTS

TABLES, EXHIBITS, AND APPENDICES

EXECUTIVE SUMMARY

DESCRIPTION

Montrose, Colorado, is a small resort community growing at a steady rate of 3% and continues to see an influx of building and development as tourism grows. As this growth continues, so does the demand for medical services. The Montrose Urgent Care Facility is a partnership of professionals that plan to provide for the shortage of after-hour medical care. It will contribute to the community by establishing the first urgent care facility in the Montrose region.

MARKET

Montrose Urgent Care Facility will have access to three markets. The primary market, Montrose County, has grown approximately 33% in the past ten years (1992–2001). Its current population is 35,000 residents and is projected to grow at a 3.4% rate. Delta, Gunnison, Ridgway, and Olathe are neighboring cities with no urgent care facilities. They provide the potential for 81,000 patient visits annually (an average market size of $12.2M). The target market for this facility are the 57% of annual medical cases that visit the local hospital emergency room, wherein the patients mainly require non-emergency attention and peace of mind. The demand for medical services in these areas is strong; there is a substantial need for an alternative to hospital emergency room medical services.

COMPETITION

There are two main medical service providers in Montrose County. The Montrose Memorial Hospital has 75 beds in a residential location and there are 14 family practitioners in the area. This urgent care clinic will provide convenience, speed of service, main road access and visibility, and cost savings for patients and insurance companies. Currently there are no direct competitors for an urgent care clinic in Montrose, Colorado.

FACILITY

The Montrose Urgent Care Facility will be built on Main Street. Medical equipment, computers, filing cabinets, office supplies, and furniture will be necessary to transform this building into a medical facility. It is 4,200 square feet and has the capacity for six examination rooms, an x-ray room, laboratory, nurse's station, business office, break room, and a patient waiting room. Hours of operation are from 4–10 p.m. each weekday and from 10 a.m.–10 p.m. on weekends.

MANAGEMENT TEAM

The management team for Montrose Urgent Care Clinic consists of doctors Tim Sullinger and Craig Tipping, both co-managing medical directors. Mark Sawyer (MBA, Notre Dame) is the project and business manager. A Webmaster and marketing consultant will be hired on contract. As demand for services increase, additional employees will be hired as needed. An advisory board will include representatives from the Montrose Memorial Hospital, economic advisory board, Rocky Mountain Health Plans (HMO), an attorney, and a CPA.

FINANCIAL INFORMATION

It is anticipated that there will be a positive cash flow by the end of year one. In five years, there will be approximately 7,000 patients per year, generating an average of $105 per visit. Revenues will increase by 20%, 17%, 15%, and 14% in years 2–5, respectively.

FUNDING REQUIREMENTS: $300,000

DESCRIPTION

MISSION STATEMENT

To improve the health and well-being of individuals in the communities we serve, providing affordable patient care with increased access, convenience, and speed. We are committed to maintaining the highest standards of clinical and service excellence, rooted in utmost integrity and moral practice.

SERVICES—URGENT CARE

Montrose Urgent Care, PLLC is a walk-in medical center for treating non–life-threatening injuries and illnesses. In essence, it is a hybrid that merges the convenience of a hospital emergency room and the cost of a family practice doctor. Montrose Urgent Care Center will be open weekdays from 4 p.m.–10 p.m. and on weekends from 10 a.m.–10 p.m. Hours of operation will be adjusted depending upon demand.

Montrose Urgent Care will provide immediate medical attention for non-emergent patients for the following conditions: illness, infections, cuts, contusions, burns, fractures, sprains, allergic reactions, accidents, and injuries. All emergency type patient visits will be directed to the Montrose Memorial Hospital ER. Emergencies include: chest pain, severe abdominal pain, difficulty breathing or shortness of breath, sudden dizziness, weakness or loss of coordination or balance, sudden blurred vision, numbness in the face, arm, or leg, sudden severe headache, deep cuts or bleeding that won't stop, coughing up or vomiting blood, severe burns or seizures.

MANAGEMENT TEAM

PARTNERS

Dr. Tim Sullinger, Co-Managing Medical Director—Dr. Sullinger received his medical degree from the Medical College of Georgia. He performed his post-doctoral training at Susquehanna Hospital in Williamsport, Pennsylvania.

He is residency trained and board certified in the state of Colorado. Over the past three years, he has developed and established a thriving medical practice in Montrose, Colorado. He has experience in an urgent care environment and is on Montrose Hospital's emergency medicine committee.

Dr. Craig Tipping—Dr. Tipping received his medical degree from the University of Health Sciences–Kansas City, Missouri. He is board certified and has been practicing medicine in Montrose, Colorado, for three years.

Both Dr. Tipping and Dr. Sullinger will continue to work as family practice physicians, but will assist partners in information gathering and facilitation of the project. Once operations begin, each physician will provide coverage at the clinic, evaluate other medical care providers, and assist in development/adherence to medical policies and procedures.

Mark Sawyer, Project and Business Manager—Mr. Sawyer is an MBA from the University of Notre Dame. Prior to that, he worked as an accountant for Arthur Andersen, LLP and PricewaterhouseCoopers, LLP.

Mr. Sawyer will be responsible for facilitating the project, including, but not limited to, business plan preparation, financing, company formation, and coordination of partnership efforts. Once the project is complete, he will manage and oversee the day-to-day operations, including staffing, accounting, financial reporting, correspondence, purchasing, etc.

ADVISORY BOARD

The advisory board will consist of Steve Sawyer, Carter Bair, David Reed, and Mary Snyder. Steve Sawyer is a surgeon in Montrose. Carter Bair is a CPA and CFO for a medically related company in Grand Junction, CO. David Reed is the mayor of Montrose and an attorney who assists many of the physicians in town. Mary Snyder is the COO of Montrose Memorial Hospital.

BUSINESS STRUCTURE

Montrose Urgent Care is incorporated under the laws of the state of Colorado as a Professional Limited Liability Company (PLLC). As with a corporation, all members of the PLLC enjoy limited personal liability. Therefore, interest in a PLLC does not normally expose the owner to legal liability for business debts and court judgments against the business, unless debts or contracts are personally guaranteed. Generally, members risk only the capital they paid into the business. Each member will share in the profits and losses equally.

Despite the formation of the PLLC, each member (physician) of the partnership is required by Colorado law to maintain personal malpractice insurance. Facility insurance will also be necessary.

MARKET RESEARCH

The medical service industry remains one of the strongest sectors in the national and Colorado economy. Cost of these services in Colorado has grown at an average annual rate of 4.4% from 1991 to 1998 (Exhibit 5). There is no anticipated change in the growth of medical service costs. The medical service sector is very price inelastic (0.7—as per R. Sheehan, Professor of Economics at the University of Notre Dame, 2003), meaning that demand for services is a necessity and, therefore, is not curbed by the economy or prices for service, etc.

Colorado health statistics show that 45% of the population will see a physician 1–3 times per year, 24% 4–9 times, and 13% will see a physician more than 10 times (1997–2000). This has been a consistent finding since 1997. As the population ages, it is expected that the demand for medical services will continue to increase as they account for the largest percentage of the population that will see a physician more than 10 times a year. The American Hospital Association has recently indicated that expected convenience in this industry is on the rise. Sixty-two percent of emergency rooms are at or over capacity (Appendix 4). In volume, it went from 86 million to 100 million cases from 1990 to 2002, respectively. There was a 5% growth in 2000–2001 alone.

MARKET DESCRIPTION

Montrose Urgent Care is based in Montrose, Colorado, and targets individuals who need immediate, flexible, and affordable medical care. Montrose Urgent Care Center will primarily service Montrose County. Montrose and Montrose County have grown approximately 33% over the past ten years (1992–2001) and are currently home to 34,596 residents.

The economic climate in the city of Montrose is good. An influx of new businesses, including a Jack Nicklaus–designed golf course and modern airport, have contributed to growth in the area. Four new physicians have been added to the region in the past year, and more are being recruited. This indicates that demand for medical services is still growing and strong.

MARKET OPPORTUNITIES

By providing flexible, convenient, after-hours non-emergent care, we can fill a void in the medical services industry. The facility will partner with local medical professionals to provide high quality, affordable services to the residents of Montrose.

Based on discussions with both family practice physicians and hospital administrators, it has been determined that there is a substantial need for an alternative to hospital ER medical services and that full support would be given to an urgent care operation.

COMPETITION

Currently, the only direct competitor to Montrose Urgent Care is Montrose Memorial Hospital's emergency room. There are three urgent care facilities located 65 miles away in Grand Junction; however, they are too far away to be considered direct competition. Indirectly, Montrose Urgent Care is competing with local physicians and their private practices.

The Montrose Memorial Hospital, at 800 S. 3rd in Montrose, is a direct competitor of the urgent care facility as we are seeking many of the cases that would otherwise go to the ER. Statistics indicate that 57% of all services performed in the emergency room are for non-emergent medical care (Appendix 4). Dr. Sullinger has met with and discussed the urgent care facility with the hospital. Based on his conversation, the hospital has given its "blessing" to go ahead with the endeavor. Potentially, this may also help the hospital as it is quickly running out of space and would need to expand its ER operations. It was made clear that they would prefer to not expand the ER at this time, as they are already engaged in another $25 million expansion project.

As the population of Montrose grows, so does the quality of service and the number of health care providers. Currently there are twelve family practice and five internal medicine physicians in Montrose. Though some patients may prefer the urgent care facility to a physician, it is anticipated that most patients will continue to see their primary care physician, visiting the center only when immediate attention is necessary. An urgent care center will help physicians in three ways: (1) Each family practice physician will have the opportunity to provide services at Montrose Urgent Care Center, for which they will be compensated. This enables physicians to "moonlight" and earn additional income. (2) As physicians participate and treat patients, they will have the opportunity to develop relationships and attract patients to their own individual practices. (3) It also provides an alternative means of treating patients after-hours and therefore minimizes the amount of time physicians must spend "on-call" seeing patients.

Both physicians and hospital services are all located off the main arteries leading into town and make it difficult for those unfamiliar with the area to locate medical services easily.

COMPETITIVE ADVANTAGES

Montrose Urgent Care maintains four main advantages over the current options for medical care: location, convenience, speed of service, and cost savings.

Location—Montrose Urgent Care is located on a main artery of town and can easily been seen from the main road. It will be very accessible to local residents or those unfamiliar with the area.

Convenience—No longer will patients with non-emergencies have to wait until their scheduled appointment to receive medical care. By visiting Montrose Urgent Care, they can receive medical care when they need it the most—immediately. In addition, because our facility will be open after hours each day of the week, most patients can visit our office after work. Appointments are not necessary when visiting the center.

Speed—Unlike typical emergency rooms, patients do not have to wait extraordinary amounts of time to be seen. Within minutes of arrival they can be escorted to a patient room and will be seen by a doctor (maximum time would be 45 minutes if four patients showed up at same time). Total time of visit is estimated to last no longer than 1 hour.

Cost Savings—Urgent care provides an affordable alternative to an ER visit. An ER visit average cost is $1,029 versus urgent care $194 (Exhibit 1). The average family physician cost is $70 for the initial visit; this does not include any additional services that may be required (e.g., tests, x-rays). See Exhibit 1 for a complete cost comparison. Montrose Urgent Care expects fees to average $135, which include the physician's services, tests, etc. In Montrose, an urgent care facility will serve to reduce costs for cash paying patients, insured patients, and insurance companies.

TARGET MARKET

A true emergency involves a medical condition of recent onset and severity that would lead a reasonable person to believe that the absence of immediate medical attention could result in one of the following:

- Placing the health of the individual in serious jeopardy.
- Serious impairment to bodily function.
- Serious dysfunction of any bodily organ or part.

Any individual who does not meet any of the above requirements is a potential patient for the Montrose Urgent Care Center. The number of visits by patients to their doctors (as stated above) was applied to the most recent census estimate data (2002) for Montrose and the surrounding area (Delta and Gunnison). Census data 2000 was used for towns Ridgeway and Olathe, as small areas are only captured in the decade census, not annually. It is a conservative estimate for these two towns due to census data 2000 not including the age 6–17-year-old market. Therefore, the total potential market for the surrounding area is slightly more attractive than the following. The potential estimated market for these counties and towns are 80,161 patients. The potential number of all non-emergency visits is 62,900. At an average cost of $194 per visit, the potential target market size is as much as $12.2 million (an estimated range is $6.5–$14.8 million, Appendix 2).

MARKETING STRATEGY

To be successful the key is to focus on the Montrose County area with an advertising and promotion campaign as well as an educational marketing campaign to develop awareness of the facility. This will be executed with all the major sources available in the area, such as other medical practitioners, employing businesses, hotels, and recreational centers. A thorough summary of available options in the area can be found in Exhibits 2 and 3. The extent of the campaign will be determined by the budget available. However, there are levels of options that can be implemented. Each component in the initial implementation is targeted to gaining awareness and acceptance and to garnering positive word of mouth. This last goal is key because in these county areas of Colorado it is the most inexpensive and effective way to develop patronage to a business.

ADVERTISING AND PROMOTION

In order to develop and solidify our position in the marketplace, we need to use marketing tools such as a Web site, billboards, brochures, press releases, local newspapers and television, and networking to inform potential customers and attract the public to our services.

Internet Web site—A Web site will be developed and provide an immediate presence on the Internet. The Web site provides a location for potential patients who surf the Web to obtain information about our services and contact information.

Billboards—A billboard will be rented and placed on Townsend and West Main Street in Montrose. It will act as a reminder of our services to future patients and help direct patients to our facility.

Brochures—Flyers and brochures describing our services, location, and contact information will be distributed to local establishments (i.e., restaurants, hotels, chamber of commerce, physician offices, etc.) in Montrose and surrounding communities.

Advertising in Local Newspapers—To develop awareness of the new facility, advertisements in the newspapers are planned.

Public Relations—We will put considerable effort into preparing and disseminating a regular flow of press releases. Releases will be based on our operations, employees, and community partnerships and published in the local paper.

Networking—We have contacted and will continue to communicate with local family practice physicians and hospital administrators to provide moral and marketing support. We will partner with these health care professionals to attract referrals and staffing support.

PRIMARY CAMPAIGN

A primary method that will be executed is pamphlets. The pamphlet's aim is to educate all potential customers to what conditions can be treated in an urgent care center and when they should use it instead of the ER. It will highlight the benefit of savings versus attending an emergency room for the same services and how utilizing this facility will lessen the overburden of the ER. These are to be provided to all avenues within the community that will allow their distribution. Key targets include the Montrose Memorial Hospital, the resident 60 private doctors, the 5 optometrists, the 20 dentists, and 8 osteopath offices. It will also include any of the financial institutions in the area that will support the business. For instance, these could include (but are not limited to) the Federal Commercial Bank, the Montrose Bank, and Wells Fargo Bank located in the downtown core. Montrose Urgent Care Center will also provide these pamphlets to any community facility that will support the awareness and educational campaign. Some of these include public golf courses/tennis courts, reservoirs, hotels, and theatres. See Exhibit 2 for an exhaustive list.

Another mandatory method of awareness will be through the use of billboards and top-of-mind awareness supplies. Several key locations along the major traffic route in and out of Montrose are targeted for this message. The message will include a simple, compelling statistic and rationale for why using the urgent care center for non-emergency reasons is the best option for patients. It will also have location and contact information displayed. To remind people of the location and contact information of the center, giveaways will be created. These include items such as printed pens, fridge magnets, stickers, stress balls, and/or a pad of paper.

Local newspapers and the company Web site will also be used as methods for disseminating further in-depth knowledge of the center. The local community paper, the *Montrose Daily Press,* is published from Sunday to Friday and is the main target for advertising the urgent care center to potential patients in the community. Other newspapers that allow free advertising for new businesses are available and will be utilized. A Web site can be tailored and updated easily to address all major, common knowledge information that residents or visitors have. It is also a way to promote interactive contact to address specific questions.

SECONDARY CAMPAIGN

The educational campaign has two additional media avenues at its disposal in Montrose County. There are three local radio stations and two local cable companies. The radio stations KKXK FM 94, KSTR FM 96.1, KJQY FM, and 102.7/KNZZ News Radio 1100 all capture the reach of the targeted listening audience. Each will be evaluated for its reach versus cost implications. The cable companies CREY TV and ATT Cablevision of Colorado are also in the Montrose area and would be able to visually reach ideal patients. A commercial for television run would need to be created and developed. This is the most expensive option available and is more likely to be implemented in the second or third year of operations when there is a positive cash flow and a percentage of income can be allocated to media coverage. Due to its broader, mass reach it also would be dollars better spent when Montrose focuses on aggressively targeting the surrounding areas of Delta, Olathe, Ridgway, and Gunnison.

FUTURE CAMPAIGN

The initial educational and awareness campaign is intended to concentrate on Montrose County. This will allow the management team to target its marketing dollars to the immediate patient audience and to measure the success and effectiveness of the campaign and individual tactics. It is important to focus efforts in the immediate area because without success in Montrose there would be no urgent care center to promote in the nearby counties. From this stage, the tools that are working best to educate and promote the urgent care center will be rolled out to Delta,

Olathe, Ridgway, and Gunnison. These areas will already be well aware of the center due to the positive reputation from word of mouth in Montrose. Further investigations into their local community centers, hotels, banks, and radio/cable stations will be explored at this time. Again, an evaluation of the costs versus reach of target audience will be used to evaluate which venue will be the best strategy to follow.

OPERATIONS

BUSINESS STRATEGY

The focus and future success of Montrose Urgent Care ultimately lies within the level of customer service it provides. Patients who have their expectations exceeded will tell their friends about the experience. At the very least, satisfied patients will return when they seek quick medical attention. The reputation of the facility will be built within the first six months of operation. Any negative experiences could severely hamper profitability of operations on a continuing basis.

In addition to the quality of service, Montrose Urgent Care's success will be determined by the support of the Montrose medical establishment. Their support is critical to our success as they will help develop Montrose Urgent Care's reputation and patient base with referrals. Currently, we have a network in place and are working with local physicians and Montrose Hospital.

CHOICE OF LOCATION AND PREMISES

We are currently in negotiations to secure a location on Main Street in Montrose, which will house the urgent care center. The location is part of a medical park that is being developed. It is ideal as it is on a main artery of town and is highly visible. It is also near the hospital and provides a quick commute in the case of a patient emergency. The location is also near numerous hotels, easy to find, and convenient for tourists visiting the area. Future development, such as a new grade school and a Target superstore, is planning to build only a few miles away, also on Main Street. This will increase the center's exposure and will aid in attracting additional patients.

The facility has 3,400 sq. ft. and encompasses six examination rooms. The facility will have an x-ray room, laboratory, nurse's station, business office, and a break room. Parking will be provided per county regulations.

HOURS OF OPERATION

Montrose Urgent Care will be open from 4 until 10 p.m. each weekday and from 10 a.m. until 10 p.m. each Saturday and Sunday. The hours will be fixed until we can ascertain accurate demand for urgent care services, at which point office hours may be adjusted.

EQUIPMENT

Substantial equipment must be purchased before opening the urgent care facility. It is anticipated that Montrose Urgent Care will need $189,009 of medical equipment to adequately equip the building. Purchased equipment will include office furniture, waiting room chairs, etc. to improve the aesthetics of the center. However, the main items necessary for purchase are a laboratory and an x-ray machine, which will account for approximately 50% of the capital expenditures (Table 8: Funding Requirements).

STAFFING/POSITIONS

In order for Montrose Urgent Care to be completely functional it needs the following positions filled: (1) physician(s), (2) registered nurse(s), (3) front desk. As demand grows, additional staffing will be required. The current staffing level will be able to service four patients per hour.

PHYSICIANS

Montrose Urgent Care requires one physician to be "in-house" during all hours of operations. A majority of the physician services will be obtained by contracting physicians within the Montrose/Delta area as well as medical residents from Grand Junction, Colorado. The contract rate for the physicians will be $50 per hour plus $10 per patient treated (average $70 per hour). Dr. Sullinger, the managing medical director, as well as Dr. Craig Tipping will provide gap coverage for nights or weekends when other physicians have failed to show or have not scheduled. During the ramp-up period Drs. Sullinger and Tipping will provide 1–2 days of service, until positive cash flow is obtained. Over the long term, we anticipate hiring a full-time physician during the week and contracting with other physicians for the weekend shift.

NURSES

Potentially many different physicians may work at Montrose Urgent Care; therefore, it is imperative that a full-time nurse be hired. The nurse's position is vital as it provides stability and continuity from day to day within the center. He/she will be a valuable source for information that will assist in streamlining operations and ensuring that proper medical care is provided. We will contract with an additional nurse to provide adequate coverage for the weekend shift. In addition, all nurses will be registered nurses and x-ray certified. This will provide a cost savings to the care center as we will not have to have a radiology technician on staff for an occasional x-ray. Also, registered nurses provide a valuable resource to physicians as they are another means of writing prescriptions for patients.

OTHER

In addition to medical professionals, we will need one full-time and one part-time receptionist. They are responsible for incoming phone calls, assisting patients with signing in and checking out, collecting cash payments, and bill submission to insurance companies.

CRITICAL RISKS

Montrose Urgent Care recognizes several risks associated with medical care in Montrose. The first is the inability to adequately educate that population and portray a high quality of medical care. The inability to do this will severely reduce our potential target market and thereby reduce our ability to generate revenues. Montrose Urgent Care recognizes this as a key to our success and will start a marketing campaign to ensure that the public is informed.

Montrose Urgent Care is always at risk of another urgent care facility opening in or around the Montrose area. However, we believe that the entity first to the market will have too strong a foothold for another facility to enter profitably, as the market will support only one urgent care facility. Another source of competition comes from other family practice physicians who may house quasi-urgent care centers out of their own offices.

Another issue may occur if Montrose Urgent Care becomes too successful, meaning that patients are perceived as being "stolen" from local practices or the ER. It may create tension within the medical community and create a political climate that is hostile toward our company. It may also reduce the number of referrals from their offices to the center. In order to reduce this risk, we are developing relations with the other physicians in town and, when possible, contracting with them to work at the center. This should increase their financial interest in the company and garner support.

FINANCIAL FORECASTS

According to the market information and information provided by management, an urgent care center will produce anywhere from $104 to $235 per patient visit (Exhibit 1). Patient visits range anywhere from 2 to 5 patients per hour. For our purposes, we have used an expected value of $135 per visit and 1.5 patient visits per hour. Also, a growth rate of 4.4% (Exhibit 5) has been incorporated for years 2–5. Patient growth of .25 patients per hour is also used for each year after year one until 2.5 patients per hour is achieved.

REVENUE

Fees from urgent care services are composed of three different categories: a physician fee, facility fee, and lab/x-ray fee. This is consistent with a hospital emergency room. A family practice physician does not receive a facility fee. Since our center will have both an x-ray and a laboratory, our fee for services will generally lie somewhere in between a family practice and an emergency room visit. The average urgent care facility bill is approximately $194 per visit (see appendix), but ranges between a low of $104 and a high of $235. Calculations use an expected value of $135 per urgent care visit. Fees anticipate a growth rate of 4.4%, which is consistent with the cost of health care in Colorado. Therefore, average fees are expected to be $141, $147, $154, and $161 in years 2–5, respectively.

Our revenue forecast is based on the assumption that 1.5 patients per hour (pph) will visit our center during the first year of operation (includes ramp-up period). The patient load will increase by .25 pph each year for the first five years and will cap out at 2.5 pph, or approximately 7,000 patients a year. In comparison, Lutheran Urgent Care in Mesa, Arizona, sees approximately 16,000 patients per year in the same size facility (however, they have a much larger population base and more competition). Additionally, family practice physicians see approximately 2–5 patients per hour.

Based on the above information, revenues will be $574,000 in year 1 and climb to $1,126,000 in year 5. Revenues will increase by 21%, 19%, 17%, and 16% over years 2–5, respectively.

INCOME STATEMENT

Based on our revenue forecast, we expect to have a net loss in year 1 of $3,000. Positive net income occurs during years 2–5 (Table 1: Income Statement). The main drivers of expenses are the substantial fixed costs that need to be serviced on a monthly basis, the largest of which is rent (triple-net) of $5,400 and salaries of $26,000 per month.

CASH FLOW PROJECTIONS

Cash flow projections (Table 4: Cash Flow Projections) show a positive cash flow at the end of year one. Cash flows for year 1 are approximately ($40,000) and reach $473,000 in year 5. In order to fund year 1, the management team will contribute $40,000 in cash and capital. Additional operating cash will be obtained through long-term financing.

Distributions are designed to compensate partners for services performed and for personal tax liabilities generated from the partnership. Future payouts will be determined by management or at the request of ownership.

RAMP-UP PERIOD

The ramp-up period will cover the first six months of operations. During this period, we anticipate a very low patient load (approximately one patient per hour). As a result, cash flows will be negative and will require adequate operating cash to fund the difference. The major cost of running urgent care is the labor cost. Therefore, to aid in the ability to obtain positive cash flows, participating management will be asked to defer their salary until positive cash flows occur (Table 6: Ramp-Up). At such point, management will have the option of receiving payment for their services and keeping it or receiving payment and lending the money back to the center. If the latter is chosen, interest will be paid to the partner on the loan.

BREAK-EVEN ANALYSIS

Break-even analysis was determined by using the low ($104), expected value ($135), and high ($235) cost per patient visits. The most likely scenario is for Montrose Urgent Care to receive an expected value of $135 per patient visit. This includes all fees (physician, facility, lab). At this rate, the center needs to see approximately 4,300 patients per year or one and one half patients per hour. Calculating the break-even analysis at the low and high fees per visit reduce the patient requirements to 2 pph and .90 pph, respectively (Table 7: Break-Even Analysis).

REQUIRED FUNDING

The management team has projected that Montrose Urgent Care requires funding of $290K (Table 8: Funding Requirements). $250K will be financed from the bank at a rate of approximately 6% over 20 years. The remaining $40K will be obtained from the founding partners. Other sources of funds, including grants and private investors, are also being pursued and may reduce the long-term bank loan.

USE OF FUNDS

We plan to make three major investments over the next 12 months: building construction, purchase of medical equipment, and start-up costs.

- Building Construction—The size of the urgent care center is approximately 3,400 square feet. We have contracted with Ridgway Construction to build the center, who will then lease the building to us for three years. The monthly lease payment will be $5,400, with an option to buy the building at a fixed price at the end of years 1, 2, or 3 (see analysis). Using this lease to buy method, we reduce the initial cash requirements for our investors/partners.
- Medical Equipment—Urgent care will require $189,009 worth of capital equipment/furniture (Table 8: Funding Requirements) and $11,991 worth of supplies. The equipment will be ordered within 60 days of completion and placed in the facility within 30 days of opening. Payment for the equipment and supplies will come through funds obtained from the investors and from a loan from the bank.
- Start-up costs are approximately $89,000, most of which is start-up cash.

INVESTOR RETURN ON INVESTMENT

In exchange for investor capital of $250,000, Montrose Urgent Care is prepared to surrender 20% ownership in the company. Outside investors can expect to receive benefits of approximately 30% return and a payback period of 4 years.

BUSINESS CONTROLS

ACCOUNTING SYSTEM

We will be using a computer-based financial management system. With this system we can review our revenue and expenses on a regular basis, analyze the profitability of the organization on a day-to-day basis, and determine staffing needs. In addition, we will be able to determine incentive payouts for doctors and staff who perform during high pph periods.

QUALITY CONTROL

We will be developing guidelines and best practices to determine the best way for medical staff to treat patients while providing high-quality, service-oriented care. Dr. Sullinger and Dr. Tipping will address issues that arise regarding patient care and risk to the practice.

We will also encourage patients to provide us with feedback regarding our services to ensure that adequate care is provided and that the patient waiting times are minimal, and to determine ways of improving services in the future.

CAPACITY

Our facility will have six separate patient rooms. Based on a maximum of four patients per hour, four rooms will accommodate all patients and will prevent long waits in the waiting room. For unusually busy times (more than four patients per hour), a waiting room will be available and can entertain up to fifteen visitors.

EXIT STRATEGY

Once profitable, Montrose Urgent Care has two main options to exit the market. It can sell to Montrose Memorial Hospital or to local medical professionals.

Since this is a medical facility, it must be sold to other medical professionals or to a hospital. Potential buyers would be Montrose Memorial Hospital or other medical professionals in the region. The hospital currently needs to expand but is unable to do so as it is already at maximum capacity in its current location. The hospital will benefit from a positive cash flow, increased services, modern equipment and facilities, and higher visibility.

Physicians in the area are also possible suitors but are unlikely as many of the candidates enjoy the ability to work separately. Emergency room doctors may have a conflict of interest with their obligations at the hospital. The best option for this alternative is young family physicians who are trying to establish themselves in the market and would like immediate cash flows without a long ramp-up period.

TIMETABLE

December 2003	PLC formation Licensing approval from Colorado State Medical Board Obtain insurance contracts—fee schedules (RMHMO and Anthem Blue Cross/ Blue Shield)
January 2004	Develop advisory board Confirm hospital support Obtain investors Sign building contract
February 2004	Begin building urgent care center
July 2004	Begin hiring process for nurses and physicians
September 2004	Begin hiring process for front office staff Furniture and equipment purchasing
October 2004	Promotion and marketing campaign Develop policies and procedures material
November 2004	Open for medical services

FINANCIAL TABLES

TABLE 1: INCOME STATEMENT—FIVE-YEAR PRO FORMA

Revenue:	FY 2005	FY 2006	FY 2007	FY 2008	FY 2009
Urgent Care Fees[1]	$574,513	$693,092	$826,958	$971,262	$1,126,664
Total Revenue	$574,513	$693,092	$826,958	$971,262	$1,126,664
Gross Profit %	100%	100%	100%	100%	100%
Operating Expenses:					
Salaries (see salaries statement)	$340,988	$347,760	$357,426	$367,224	$377,162
Guaranteed Payments[2]	–	–	–	–	–
Repairs and Maintenance[3]	6,000	6,000	6,000	6,000	6,000
Bad Debts[4]	17,235	20,793	24,809	29,138	33,800
Rent[5]	64,800	64,800	64,800	64,800	64,800
Taxes and Licenses[6]	7,524	7,690	7,891	8,102	8,323
Interest – Bank[7]	14,950	14,581	14,155	13,702	13,221
Interest – Partners		8,897	12,897	12,897	12,897
Depreciation/Amortization[8]	30,239	30,239	30,239	30,239	30,239
Other Expenses (see statement)	95,748	105,567	112,595	120,171	128,330
Total Operating Expenses	$577,483	$606,326	$630,811	$652,273	$674,771
Operating Expense as % of Sales	100.52%	87.48%	76.28%	67.16%	59.89%
Net Operating Income	$(2,971)	$86,766	$196,147	$318,989	$451,893
Net Income (Loss) as % of Sales	−0.52%	12.52%	23.72%	32.84%	40.11%

Assumptions:

1 Year 1—2 patients per hour, $135 per visit—Increasing .25 pph and increasing fees 4% per visit
2 None
3 $500 per month above triple net
4 3% of Sales
5 $5,400 per month per contract with Ridgway Real Estate
6 Payroll taxes for 3 employees, all others are contract labor
7 $250,000 20-year bank note, financed at 6%
8 Straight line depreciation

TABLE 2: OTHER EXPENSES

Other Expenses:	FY 2005	FY 2006	FY 2007	FY 2008	FY 2009
Advertising[1]	$24,000	$24,000	$24,000	$24,000	$24,000
Benefits (employee health)[2]	18,000	18,000	18,000	18,000	18,000
Billing[3]	19,150	25,991	31,011	36,422	42,250
Equipment Rent[4]	–	–	–	–	–
Insurance[5]	12,000	12,000	12,000	12,000	12,000
Dues & Subcriptions[6]	480	480	480	480	480
Office Expenses[7]	4,800	4,800	4,800	4,800	4,800
Professional Fees[8]	1,500	1,500	1,500	1,500	1,500
Supplies Expense[9]	4,800	6,000	6,000	6,000	6,000
Miscellaneous[10]	8,618	10,396	12,404	14,569	16,900
Telephone[11]	2,400	2,400	2,400	2,400	2,400
Utilities[12]	–	–	–	–	–
	$6,579	$7,538	$8,437	$8,557	$8,857

Assumptions:

1 Allotment per management
2 $500 per month maximum per employee covered (3)
3 5% of revenue per Southwest Billing
4 None
5 Estimated at $1,000 per month
6 For professional magazines as well as waiting room magazines
7 $400 per month for miscellaneous paper and forms expense
8 Fees for partnership and personal tax returns
9 Restocking of supplies of approximately 50% per year
10 Miscellaneous expense is estimated to be .15% of revenue
11 Estimated
12 Utilities included in triple-net payment of $5,400

TABLE 3: SALARIES

Salaries Expense:			FY 2004	FY 2005	FY 2006	FY 2007	FY 2008
Physician[1]	$50	(p/hr)	$184,275	$189,540	$196,560	$203,580	$210,600
Nurse–RN[2]	$25	(p/hr)	70,875	70,200	70,200	70,200	70,200
Radiology Tech[3]	$ 0	(p/hr)	-	-	-	-	-
Employee–Administrator[4]			50,400	52,920	55,566	58,344	61,262
Employee–Bonus[5]	0.3		-	-	-	-	-
Employee–Front Desk/Secretary[6]	12.5	(p/hr)	35,438	35,100	35,100	35,100	35,100
			$340,988	$347,760	$357,426	$367,224	$377,162

Assumptions:

1 Physicians contract rate of $50 per hour, plus $10 per patient (54 hours per week)
2 RN contract rate of $25 per hour (54 hours per week)
3 None, depending on skills of RN
4 $50,000 per contract with a 5% rate increase each year
5 30% of cash flows
6 Front desk contract rate of $12.50 per hour (54 hours per week)

TABLE 4: CASH FLOWS

Cash Flow from Operations:	FY 2005	FY 2006	FY 2007	FY 2008	FY 2009
Net Income:	$(2,971)	$86,766	$196,147	$318,989	$451,893
Change in A/R	(61,840)	–	–	–	–
Non-Cash Expenditures:					
Depreciation/Amortization	$30,239	$30,239	$30,239	$30,239	$30,239
Total	$30,239	$30,239	$30,239	$30,239	$30,239
Reportable Cash Expenditures:					
Financing–Principal Only	$6,543	$6,912	$7,338	$7,791	$8,271
Total	$6,543	$6,912	$7,338	$7,791	$8,271
Other Cash Outflows:					
Capital Purchases	–	–	–	–	–
Loan Principal	–	–	–	–	–
Owners' Draw	–	–	–	–	–
Total	–	–	–	–	–
Other Cash Inflows:					
Partner's Contribution	$111,211	$50,000	–	–	–
Ending Cash Balance	$144,796	$304,889	$523,936	$865,373	$1,339,234
Beginning Cash Balance:	$74,700	$144,796	$304,889	$523,936	$865,373
Total Cash Flow	70,096	160,093	219,047	341,437	473,860

TABLE 5: BALANCE SHEET—FIVE YEAR PRO FORMA

ASSETS:		Start-Up	FY 2004	FY 2005	FY 2006	FY 2007	FY 2008
Current Assets:							
Cash		$74,700	$144,796	$304,889	$523,936	$865,373	$1,339,234
Accounts Receivable		–	61,840	61,840	61,840	61,840	61,840
Supplies Inventory		11,991	11,991	11,991	11,991	11,991	11,991
Total Current Assets		$86,691	$218,627	$378,720	$597,767	$939,204	$1,413,065
Long-Term Assets:							
Computers		$6,604	$5,283	$3,962	$2,642	$1,321	–
Less: Depr. Expense	5yr	–	1,321	1,321	1,321	1,321	1,321
Exam Equipment–							
Urgent Care		173,295	148,539	123,782	99,026	74,269	49,513
Less: Depr. Expense	7yr	–	24,756	24,756	24,756	24,756	24,756
Furniture & Fixtures		9,110	7,809	6,507	5,206	3,904	2,603
Less: Depr. Expense	7yr	–	1,301	1,301	1,301	1,301	1,301
Start-Up Costs		14,300	11,440	8,580	5,720	2,860	–
Less: Depr. Expense	5yr	–	2,860	2,860	2,860	2,860	2,860
Total Fixed Assets		$203,309	$173,070	$142,832	$112,593	$82,354	$52,116
Total Assets		290,000	391,697	521,551	710,360	1,021,558	1,465,180
Liabs & P/E:							
Long-term Liabilities							
Long-Term NP–Bank		$250,000	$243,457	$236,545	$229,207	$221,416	$213,145
Long-Term NP–Officer		–	111,211	161,211	161,211	161,211	161,211
Total Long-Term Liabilities		$250,000	$354,668	$397,756	$390,418	$382,627	$374,356
Total Liabilities		$250,000	$354,668	$397,756	$390,418	$382,627	$374,356
Owners' Equity							
Owners' Equity		$40,000	$40,000	$37,029	$123,795	$319,942	$638,932
Owners' Distribution		–	–	–	–	–	–
Net Income		–	(2,971)	86,766	196,147	318,989	451,893
Total Owners' Equity		$40,000	$37,029	$123,795	$319,942	$638,932	$1,090,825
Total P/E & Liabilities		$290,000	$391,697	$521,551	$710,360	$1,021,558	$1,465,180

TABLE 6: RAMP-UP

Assumptions:	FY 2004	FY 2005	FY 2006	FY 2007	FY 2008
# of visits - Urgent Care (per hour)	1.50	1.75	2.00	2.25	2.50
# of operating hours (week)	54	54	54	54	54
$ per patient visit	$135	$141.04	$147.25	$153.73	$160.49
Total Patients Per Year	4,212	4,914	5,616	6,318	7,020
Bad Debt Rate	3.00%				

Operating Hours of Urgent Care (M–F 4–10 pm & weekends 10–10 pm) Per Week

Ramp Up:

	January	February	March	April	May	June
Patients Per Hour	0.5	1.25	1.25	1.5	1.5	1.5
$ Per Patient	$135	$135	$135	$135	$135	$135
Hours Per Month	236	236	236	236	236	236
Total Revenue	$15,959	$39,897	$39,897	$47,876	$47,876	$47,876
Cash Receipts						
Month 1: 25% Cash Payers	$3,990	$9,974	$9,974	$11,969	$11,969	$11,969
Month 2: 50% Insured		7,979	19,948	19,948	23,938	23,938
Month 3: 25% Other			3,990	9,974	9,974	11,969
Total Cash Flow	$3,990	$17,954	$33,912	$41,892	$45,881	$47,876
Cash Disbursements						
Salaries (see salaries statement)	$26,053	$27,825	$27,825	$28,416	$28,416	$28,416
Repairs and Maintenance[3]	500	500	500	500	500	500
Bad Debts[4]	479	1,197	1,197	1,436	1,436	1,436
Rent[5]	5,400	5,400	5,400	5,400	5,400	5,400
Taxes and Licenses[6]	544	544	544	544	544	544
Bank Note	1,791	1,791	1,791	1,791	1,791	1,791
Other Expenses (see statement)	7,379	8,337	9,235	9,354	7,253	7,253
Total Operating Cash Flows	$42,146	$45,594	$46,491	$47,441	$45,340	$45,340
Net Cash Flows	(38,156)	(27,640)	(12,579)	(5,549)	541	2,536
Beginning Cash	74,700	45,032	26,464	22,958	26,676	36,485
Deferred Salaries	8,488	9,073	9,073	9,268	9,268	9,268
Ending Cash	45,032	26,464	22,958	26,676	36,485	48,288

TABLE 6: RAMP-UP (CONTINUED)

Ramp-Up:

	July	August	September	October	November	December	Total
Patients Per Hour	1.5	1.75	1.75	1.75	1.75	2	1.5
$ Per Patient	$135	$135	$135	$135	$135	$135	$135
Hours Per Month	236	236	236	236	236	236	2,835
Total Revenue	$47,876	$55,855	$55,855	$55,855	$55,855	$63,835	$574,513
Cash Receipts							
Month 1: 25% Cash Payers	$11,969	$13,964	$13,964	$13,964	$13,964	$15,959	
Month 2: 50% Insured	23,938	23,938	27,928	27,928	27,928	27,928	
Month 3: 25% Other	11,969	11,969	11,969	13,964	13,964	13,964	
Total Cash Flow	$47,876	$49,871	$53,861	$55,855	$55,855	$57,850	$512,673
Cash Disbursements							
Salaries (see salaries statement)	$28,416	$29,006	$29,006	$29,006	$29,006	$29,597	$340,988
Repairs and Maintenance[3]	500	500	500	500	500	500	6,000
Bad Debts[4]	1,436	1,676	1,676	1,676	1,676	1,915	17,235
Rent[5]	5,400	5,400	5,400	5,400	5,400	5,400	64,800
Taxes and Licenses[6]	544	544	544	544	544	1,544	7,524
Bank Note	1,791	1,791	1,791	1,791	1,791	1,791	21,493
Other Expenses (see statement)	7,253	7,373	7,672	7,672	7,672	9,292	95,748
Total Operating Cash Flows	$45,340	$46,290	$46,589	$46,589	$46,589	$50,039	$553,788
Net Cash Flows	$2,536	$3,581	$7,272	$9,266	$9,266	$7,812	$(41,115)
Beginning Cash	48,288	60,092	73,135	89,869	108,598	127,327	739,625
Deferred Salaries	9,268	9,462	9,462	9,462	9,462	9,657	111,211
Ending Cash	60,092	73,135	89,869	108,598	127,327	144,796	809,721

TABLE 7: BREAK-EVEN ANALYSIS

Break-Even Analysis–Worst Case

	Total Expenses	Revenue per Visit	Number of Patients	Patients per Hour	Anticipated Patients per Hour
2004	$577,483	$104.00	5,553	1.98	1.50
2005	$606,326	$108.58	5,584	1.99	1.75
2006	$630,811	$113.35	5,565	1.98	2.00
2007	$652,273	$118.34	5,512	1.96	2.25
2008	$674,771	$123.55	5,462	1.95	2.50

Break-Even Analysis–Expected Value (Probable Case)

	Total Expenses	Revenue per Visit	Number of Patients	Patients per Hour	Anticipated Patients per Hour
2004	$577,483	$135.00	4,278	1.52	1.50
2005	$606,326	$140.94	4,302	1.53	1.75
2006	$630,811	$147.14	4,287	1.53	2.00
2007	$652,273	$153.62	4,246	1.51	2.25
2008	$674,771	$160.37	4,207	1.50	2.50

Break-Even Analysis–Best Case

	Total Expenses	Revenue per Visit	Number of Patients	Patients per Hour	Anticipated Patients per Hour
2004	$577,483	$235.00	2,457	0.88	1.50
2005	$606,326	$245.34	2,471	0.88	1.75
2006	$630,811	$256.13	2,463	0.88	2.00
2007	$652,273	$267.40	2,439	0.87	2.25
2008	$674,771	$279.17	2,417	0.86	2.50

TABLE 8: SUMMARY OF FUNDING REQUIREMENTS

Summary of Funding Requirements	
Supplies	$11,991
Start-up Costs	14,300
Start-up Cash	69,300
Mortgage Payment (1st Month)	5,400
Equipment	189,009
	$290,000

APPENDIX 1: SWOT ANALYSIS

Strengths

- Team members—management
- Knowledge of process
- Familiarity with Colorado area
- Network of doctors
- High barrier to entry (expensive)
- First mover advantage; other larger players are not financially interested in the small, niche market
- Patients have less wait time, are less annoyed
- Small community area—good word of mouth will help grow business
- Costs less than emergency room or family practitioners
- Location—easy access versus hospital
- Different hours than local doctors

Weaknesses

- Limited resources, i.e., staffing, money
- Bad word of mouth—just takes one case
- Initial capacity
- High fixed costs

Opportunity

- Reduce health fees
- Expansion to similar areas
- Expansion of additional services (dentist, chiropractor, etc.)
- Improved community services
- Reduce pressure for emergency facility, improved efficiency

Threats

- Other physicians in the area
- Political instability, i.e., hospital, Rocky Mountain HMO

APPENDIX 2: MARKET ATTRACTIVENESS CALCULATIONS

2002 Census Data Estimates

		Number of Visits			
	Est	None	1 to 3	4 to 9	10+
Montrose					
Under 5 years	2,419	152.397	1,071.617	926.477	270.928
6-17 years	6,756	1,020.156	3,931.992	2,587.548	756.672
18 years to 64	20,816	7,951.712	18,463.792	9,346.384	5,828.48
65 years and over	5,323	404.548	1,708.683	1,948.218	1,261.551
Delta					
Under 5 years	1,537	96.831	680.891	588.671	172.144
6-17 years	5,155	778.405	3,000.21	1,974.365	577.36
18 years to 64	16,571	6,330.122	14,698.477	7,440.379	4,639.88
65 years and over	5,653	429.628	1,814.613	2,068.998	1,339.761
Olathe					
Under 5 years	158	9.954	69.994	60.514	17.696
18 years to 64	852	325.464	755.724	382.548	238.56
65 years and over	220	16.72	70.62	80.52	52.14
Ridgway					
Under 5 years	45	2.835	19.935	17.235	5.04
18 years to 64	468	178.776	415.116	210.132	131.04
65 years and over	40	3.04	12.84	14.64	9.48
Gunnison					
Under 5 years	784	49.392	347.312	300.272	87.808
6-17 years	1,790	270.29	1,041.78	685.57	200.48
18 years to 64	10,549	4,029.718	9,356.963	4,736.501	2,953.72
65 years and over	1,025	77.9	329.025	375.15	242.925
Total		22,127.888	57,789.584	33,744.122	18,785.67

Overall Visits	110,319.371	
Non-Emergent Cases	0.57	
	62,882.04147	

Average Cost/Case	Low	Average	High
	104	194	235
Potential Revenues	$6,539,732.31	$ 12,199,116.05	$ 14,777,279.75

*there is money to be made!!!

Note: Estimates are only provided for counties, not towns.
Therefore the 2000 census data for Olathe and Ridgway are used, and ages 6–17 are not included.
Source: http://www.factfinder.census.gov

B BETTER BUSINESS PLAN COMPETITIONS

A wide variety of business plan competitions are held worldwide. Listed in this appendix are some of the better known competitions as compiled by SmallBusinessNotes.com.

Asian Moot Corp
Competition among the graduate business programs in Asia. The winner of the Moot Corp competition at the University of Texas represents the United States at this event.

Babson College Business Plan Competition
Separate undergraduate and graduate student events.

Bank One Business Competition
Participants must be students in the Business Plan Preparation Course at the University of Colorado–Boulder.

Bioscience Business Plan Competition
Open to academics, postdoctoral scientists, and PhD students in all United Kingdom universities and Biotechnology and Biological Sciences Research Council–sponsored research institutes.

Burton D. Morgan Entrepreneurship Competition
All Purdue University students are eligible to participate in the event. Nonstudents—such as students from other colleges, Purdue alumni, and local residents—can also be team members, but Purdue students must make the final presentations to the judges.

Case-Weatherhead Business Launch Competition
Participants must have a technology-based business concept and have at least one team member who is affiliated with Case Western Reserve University as a student, faculty member, or alumnus.

Ceem Business Plan Competition
Open to all currently registered University of California–Santa Barbara students.

CIBC Ivey Business Plan Competition
Open to teams of two to six MBA students enrolled in an accredited Canadian university.

The Duke Start-up Challenge
Each team must include one full-time student in any program at Duke University.

E-Challenge

All Stanford University students, research and postdoctoral staff, and faculty are eligible to enter the Stanford Entrepreneur's Challenge. Although individuals not affiliated with Stanford University are encouraged to participate, any entering team must have at least half its members affiliated with Stanford University.

Eureka!

The B-Plan competition of Indian Institute of Technology, Bombay. At least one member of the team must be a student. The student can be of any college or any university.

First Capital Challenge

$50,000 competition for the best plan to start a high-potential business in Kingston, Ontario, Canada. Open to anyone, anywhere.

Global Social Venture Competition

Students must create business plans that demonstrate both economic and social value. Each team must have an actively involved, current MBA student from any business school in the United States or abroad.

Great Lakes Entrepreneur's Quest

Any person or group that has a business concept focused in or based on technology (such as an e-commerce platform, a life sciences application, or an advanced manufacturing breakthrough) can compete in the business plan competition. Each team must include at least one member who resides, works, or attends school in Michigan.

GSAS Harvard Biotechnology Club Business Plan Competition

Open to entrepreneurs, students, and professionals worldwide and does not require Harvard University affiliation. The competition offers a $5,000 cash award for the first prize, a $1,000 cash award for second prize, and an opportunity for early-stage biotechnology companies to have their business plans reviewed by seasoned venture capitalists focused on this industry and other biotechnology experts in the Boston area.

Harvard Business School Business Plan Competition

Every team must have a minimum of one Harvard Business School second-year student.

The Marriott School Business Plan Competition

Open to Brigham Young University students.

Maximum Exposure Business Plan Competition

Participating teams must consist of at least one current New York University Leonard N. Stern School of Business MBA student. The competition is also known as the Stern $50K Plus.

The MIT $50K Entrepreneurship Competition

All full-time and part-time Massachusetts Institute of Technology students at all levels of education and from any department, registered with MIT for the current semester, are eligible to enter.

The Moot Corp Competition

One of the original competitions. MBAs from business schools around the globe come to the University of Texas at Austin each year to present their business plans to panels of investors.

New Venture Challenge
Each team is required to have at least one student from the Graduate School of Business, University of Chicago. This includes campus, part-time, evening, or weekend students.

New Venture Champion
Interuniversity competition sponsored by the University of Oregon.

Oxford University Business Plan Competition
Open to anyone with an imaginative idea for creating a new business. Located in Oxford, England.

Palo Alto Software Business Planning Competition
Contestants must submit plans that are for a new business that has been running less than one year, or for an expansion of an existing business. All plans must be in Business Plan Pro format.

Rice University Business Plan Competition
Hosted by the Rice Alliance for Technology and Entrepreneurship, the Rice University Business Plan competition is open to graduate student teams from all universities who are interested in funding their company.

Syracuse Business Plan Competition
Open to all graduate and undergraduate students enrolled at Syracuse University. Students must have been enrolled during at least one semester of the current academic year. More than $40,000 in prizes are awarded to the top three teams. Help sessions are available to teams through the Business Plan Laboratory. Intents to compete can be submitted online.

The SkiView Business Plans Competition
An in-house competition for students from the University of Arizona enrolled in the Berger Entrepreneurship Program.

Tech Valley Collegiate Business Plan Competition
Open to all full-time registered students in a college or university located within the nineteen-county Tech Valley region. Cash and prizes total $50,000.

UC Berkeley Business Plan Competition
A self-funded, student-run competition open to ventures run by University of California at Berkeley students and alumni.

UMass Lowell $10K Business Plan Competition
Open to all currently registered University of Massachusetts–Lowell students and alumni within one year of their graduation.

University of Notre Dame Mendoza College of Business Gigot Center Business Plan Competitions
Open to undergraduates, graduate students, and alumni of the University of Notre Dame. Competitions include the McCloskey For-Profit Competition, the Social Venture Division, the Dorothy Dolphin Family Business Competition, and the Invention Convention.

University of San Francisco International Business Plan Competition
The competition is open to graduate students from all universities and features a judging panel of Silicon Valley venture capitalists and $25,000 in cash prizes.

University of Washington Business Plan Competition

Open to students who are enrolled in degree-seeking programs at Washington State University, Seattle Pacific University, Pacific Lutheran University, Seattle University, and the University of Washington.

V. Dale Cozad Business Plan Contest

Open to all persons eighteen years and older. Additionally, at least one member of each team must be a full-time student of the University of Illinois at Urbana-Champaign and be in good standing during the duration of the competition.

Venture Adventure

An undergraduate business plan competition hosted by the Center for Entrepreneurial & Family Enterprises at Colorado State University.

Venture Challenge

The San Diego State University Business Plan Competition is open to all students currently enrolled or enrolled during the calendar year prior to the competition.

Wharton Business Plan Competition

Any student(s) in any school of the University of Pennsylvania are eligible to participate as individuals or on teams. At least one member of each team must be an active student at the University of Pennsylvania (graduate or undergraduate). Partnerships between students and nonstudents are eligible.

WPI Venture Forum Business Plan Contest

To be eligible, business plans must involve technology-based ventures and describe the development of a new product, a new application or process in an existing business, or the start-up of a new business.

Y50K Yale Entrepreneurship Competition

A universitywide business plan competition that provides start-up funding as well as educational, networking, and mentoring opportunities to Yale University entrepreneurs.

INDEX